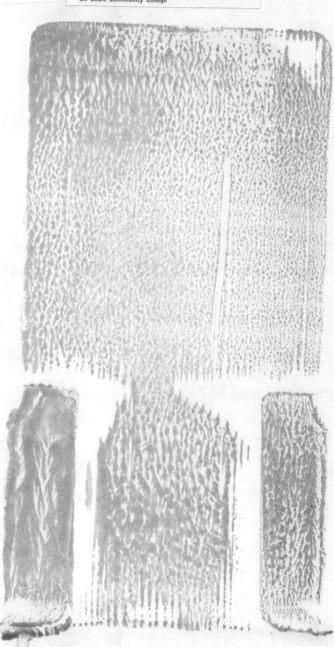

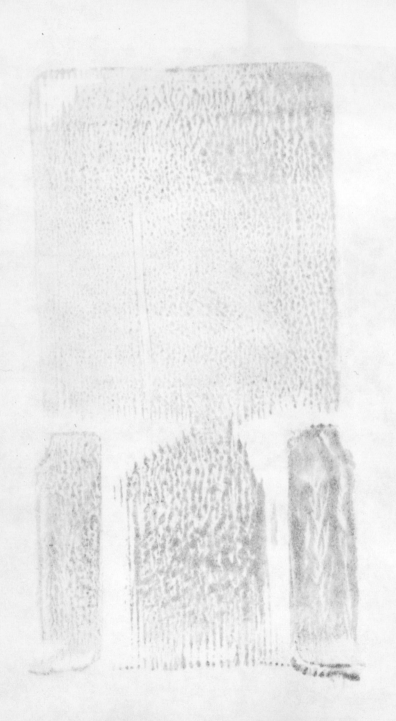

Piety along the Potomac

Piety

along the Potomac

Notes on
Politics and Morals
in the Fifties

WILLIAM LEE MILLER

The Riverside Press Cambridge
HOUGHTON MIFFLIN COMPANY BOSTON

1964

SOURCES

Most of the essays in this book have previously appeared, often in somewhat different form, in various magazines and books:

The Reporter: "The Liking of Ike," "Eisenhower, Moralist" (under the title "Religion, Politics and the Great Crusade"), "An Unspecific Discussion Not Dealing in Personalities," "Piety along the Potomac," "The Bipartisanship of Vicunas," "Politics Is So Confusing," "Can Government Be Merchandised?", "Our Sins Are Your Fault" (under the title "Should We Fight Dirty, Too?"), "The Debating Career of Richard M. Nixon," "Some Negative Thinking about Norman Vincent Peale," "The Irony of Reinhold Niebuhr," "The Moral Force behind Dulles' Diplomacy," "Weapons in the Web of Politics" (under the title "Nuclear Morality"). Copyright 1953, 1954, 1955 by The Fortnightly Publishing Co., Inc.; Copyright © 1956, 1958, 1962 by The Reporter Magazine Company.

Episcopal Churchnews: "The Corruption of Corruption." Copyright 1953 by The Southern Churchman Co.

Christianity and Crisis: "From Suasion to Dissuasion," "The End of the Middle of the Road." Copyright © 1958, 1959 by *Christianity and Crisis.*

The World Alliance Newsletter: "The People and Foreign Policy." Copyright © 1958 by The Church Peace Union.

Confluence: "The Religious Revival and American Politics." Copyright © 1955 by The President and Fellows of Harvard College.

East-West Negotiations: "The American Mind and World Realities." Copyright © 1958 by Washington Center of Foreign Policy Research.

Alliance Policy in the Cold War, edited by Arnold Wolfers, Johns Hop-

For Betty Lou

Acknowledgments

MY CHIEF debt, for this book, is to *The Reporter*, in which much of the material in it first appeared, and to Max Ascoli, the editor of that magazine. I am indebted to him, and also to Douglass Cater and Robert Bingham and others of the staff of *The Reporter*, for many improvements and many ideas. *The Reporter* has kindly given its permission to reprint the articles from its pages.

I am grateful also to Mrs. Anne Barrett of Houghton Mifflin Company for much assistance in putting the book together, and for patient encouragement while waiting for it, both going far beyond the call of a publisher's duty.

I have a debt going beyond anything reflected in this book to my former colleagues at the Washington Center for Foreign Policy Research, and especially to the director, and my former teacher, Arnold Wolfers. They have given much help on some of these essays, especially the ones on foreign policy.

Betty Horton Miller typed and criticized most of the material in this book, and encouraged the author mightily on many occasions through the years of its composition. I am happy to dedicate the book, inadequate though it is for such a presentation, to her.

W.L.M.

Contents

Part III

Part IV

Part V

Introduction: The Fifties

THIS BOOK deals with a distinct feature of the decade just past, the intersection of popular ideas about moral values with American politics. It deals also, in a minor way, with modern devices of political publicity and with the revived religious interest — two other prominent features of the time — where these pass through that point of intersection. Putting these several features together — they are obviously related to each other — shows, I think, one obtrusive aspect of the fifties.

Or rather, of the Eisenhower years. Commentators and popular historians find it convenient when history groups its periods to correspond to the decades of the calendar — as in the twenties and the thirties it almost perfectly did — but we cannot always have it that way. History did not quite oblige us in the 1950's, although it almost did. The early years of that decade, when Mr. Truman was President, and the Korean war was being fought, and Senator McCarthy was making himself inescapable, must be separated from what came later. The symbolic fifties did not begin until the "Great Moral Crusade" of 1952; they became more distinct after Stalin died, and the Korean war ended, and then later Senator McCarthy was made to subside. The high point of the characteristic spirit of this time may have come around 1955, when long cars with tailfins were selling in record numbers, and *The Power of Positive*

Thinking was the best seller, and the Spirit of Geneva diffused itself briefly over the globe. The year 1956 and much of 1957 had something of the same mood, but later on cars became shorter and thinking less positive. The Russian Sputnik in the fall of 1957 struck the major blow to the spirit of the fifties, and before and after it other blows were struck. The last years of the fifties saw the characteristic spirit of the period diminish. The decade that began with querulous accusations about "corruption" and subversion ended with troubled self-accusations about "national purpose" and "national goals." Somewhere in between, however, there was a brief happy moment when a combination of prosperity, Eisenhower, peace, religiosity, moral language, nostalgic patriotism, and public relations brought a precarious plateau of repose to many characteristic Americans.

Some of the country's more or less permanent moral attitudes toward politics were reflected in that moment. Behind the broad politics of the day there is the broad culture of the day, and behind the broad culture of the day are the more or less enduring values of a people. Behind the politics of the fifties there was the peculiar spirit of the time, and behind that there were some perennial American traits and convictions. The spirit of the time, as I have said, was one of attempted repose, after the energetic efforts of the depression and the New Deal, the second war, the shaping of the cold war 1946–1950, and the Korean war. In such a time some semi-conservative values of the people showed through.

The appraisals that follow are not, as an alert reader will quickly realize, altogether objective descriptions of this subject — the spirit of the fifties. They contain a large ingredient of criticism. The fifties did not, in my opinion, show the American people at their worst (except in the McCarthy episode, which subsided and was not characteristic of what came later) but they also did not show us at our best: rather they showed us at something like a counterfeit of our best. There was a great yearning effort to reflect a sound Americanism, and a moral substance, and also — not as much in a separate category as it ought to be — religious conviction. But these higher yearnings had no critical edge. They did not unsettle conventional opinions. They required little significant new effort either of thought or of action.

The best of Americanism is the democratic idealism that (as we say toward the end of speeches) has made our country great. The fifties had a slight touch of that idealism, but it was very slight, and it was joined to our moralistic misunderstanding (as it seems to me) of politics, of social interdependence, and of government. It is curious that a people so devoted to "democracy" (a form of politics and of government) should be at the same time so suspicious of politics and of government. It is further curious that that suspicion should sometimes be most prominent when a conscious moral idealism is set forth. But of that, more in the essays that follow. They may be read either as a partial picture of the politics of the time, or as discussions of the topic (moral values and American politics) that the time brought into view.

Part I

The Liking of Ike*

IN 1952 Dwight Eisenhower received the largest number of votes until then ever given any presidential candidate in American history — nearly thirty-four million of them. His name on the ballot helped to draw to the polls the largest number of voters ever to participate in the American presidential election — nearly twelve million more than the previous record, nearly thirteen million more than in 1948. A highly placed Democrat grumpily and privately observed that the 1952 total apparently included votes from millions who had never voted before — and he would be as happy if they never voted again.

But they did. In 1956 Mr. Eisenhower's margin over his opponent was nearly ten million votes; he topped his own record by winning the votes of over thirty-five million Americans, more than eight million more than any other person running for the Presidency had then received, and more than his successor won from the enlarged electorate. He carried Chicago; Montgomery, Alabama; and even Jersey City — places that were venerable bulwarks of Democratic strength. A disgruntled Democrat said, somewhat ungraciously, that they

---

* This article was published in *The Reporter* on October 16, 1958, but I have added some material and subtracted some other material and changed the tense.

seemed to be coming up out of the woodwork to vote for Mr. Eisenhower.

These victories were of a size that can comfortably bear all the explanations we can muster, both those that draw upon objective historical conditions, like peace and prosperity, and those that deal in the more elusive realms of culture, character, and personality. But the latter were especially important. Peace and prosperity, "Korea, Corruption, and Communism," were not as central to those elections as, simply, the liking of Ike.

Mr. Eisenhower not only won his races easily; he won them while the partisan tide was running against him. While he was consistently winning elections, his party was just as consistently losing them. In 1952 the party's congressional candidates ran over five million votes — and 15 percent — behind him; in 1954 they lost control of Congress. In 1956, Mr. Eisenhower ran ahead of his party's candidates for Congress by the astounding total of ten million votes. For the only time in modern party history and the first time since 1848, the victorious candidate for President failed to carry his party to control of Congress with him. In 1958 that party lost Congress again, and overwhelmingly. In 1954, 1956, 1958: for the first time in American history a President faced three Congresses controlled by the opposing party. The Eisenhower years were not Republican years.

Mr. Eisenhower claimed on the evening of his 1956 victory that the election showed the country accepted "modern Republicanism." But that is not what the Eisenhower elections showed. They did not demonstrate that the American people liked Mr. Eisenhower's party, ancient or modern; they showed only that the American people liked Mr. Eisenhower himself.

The attraction of President Eisenhower transcended the

conditions of the time in which it was tested at the polls. One study of his political appeal, going back to 1947, concluded that, on the evidence, it was "highly probable that Eisenhower could have been elected President on either major party ticket in either 1948 or 1952." *

A unique and motley list of national leaders, presumably sensitive to public desires, urged General Eisenhower's candidacy for the Presidency on the ticket of one party or the other, in the years before the 1948 election: Alfred M. Landon and Franklin Roosevelt, Jr.; Senator Claude Pepper and Senator John Stennis; Adolph Berle and Frank Hague; James B. Carey of the CIO, and Senator Richard Russell of Georgia; Jake Arvey, who said — an interesting sidelight to future events — that Adlai Stevenson might put Mr. Eisenhower's name in nomination — and also, Senator John Sparkman. The polls clearly showed his great popularity in all segments of the population: in late 1947, he ran well ahead of President Truman in a trial heat conducted by George Gallup; later, he ran ahead of Governor Dewey among Republicans. He was consistently the first choice of independent voters; his name was mentioned more often than any other as the voters' spontaneous choice for the Presidency in a three-state poll made in 1948. He drew this immense political support despite the facts: "(a) It was not known which party claimed his sympathies, (b) he had made no major pronouncements on the outstanding issues of the time, and (c) he had strongly emphasized his unavailability for the nomination." This study concludes: "If this analysis is correct, it is implied that the issues . . . over which the 1952 campaign was fought, were decidedly less important than was the simple candidacy of Dwight D. Eisenhower."

* Herbert H. Hyman and Paul B. Sheatsley, "The Political Appeal of President Eisenhower," *Public Opinion Quarterly*, Winter 1953–54.

The issues did have some importance in the presidential elections of 1952 and 1956, but that importance would have been
drastically reduced had any other Republican than Mr. Eisenhower been the nominee.

Though the Korean war was of large political significance,
its full potency did not rest in the "stalemate" alone; it lay in
the presumed ability of the man Dwight D. Eisenhower to do
something about it — in the word that voters often used, to
"handle" the situation. As the Report of the Survey Research
Center said, the Korean war "was much more a pro-Eisenhower
than a pro-Republican issue." It was the association of this man
with the problem that made the Korean war an especially big
loser for the Democrats. In Mr. Eisenhower's announcement
that "I will make that trip; I will go to Korea" the word "I" was
just as important as the word "Korea": the connection of the
two made the effect. It was Ike who would make the trip, and
without him it would not be the same.

In 1956 voters showed even more strikingly that it was not
just peace, but Ike and peace, that they found really persuasive.
When, in the last weeks of the campaign, the "peace" was
shattered by tumultuous events in Europe and the Middle East,
this fact worked not against Mr. Eisenhower, but for him. The
voters were attached not just to peace, but to the peacemaker.
To the frustration of the Democrats, he won either way; the
peace, when it existed, was of his making: the peace, when it
was in danger, was his to keep.

The other important condition that helped the Republicans,
a prosperous, middle class nation's satisfaction with a "moderate" approach to domestic problems, also depended on Mr.
Eisenhower's own personal appeal to become fully effective.

The suburbs and the middle class were also big and important in 1948; the mood of the country then might have been

described as "moderate"; Governor Dewey represented positions similar to those that Mr. Eisenhower was to represent — but Dewey lost, and Eisenhower won, and the difference between the Republican vote for Dewey in 1948 (twenty-one million) and for Eisenhower in 1952 (thirty-three million) is striking. The ticket splitting in both of the Eisenhower elections suggests that "moderation" or conservatism was hardly the whole story. Moderate, Eisenhower Republicans did not necessarily fare better than other Republicans. Liberal Democrats did not necessarily fare worse than more "moderate" ones. Mr. Eisenhower cut across all that. He not only carried the suburbs, but he carried the cities. He not only took Lake Forest and Libertyville; he also took Chicago. Mr. Eisenhower's was a national victory, making deep inroads into traditional Democratic groups.

If millions of Americans voted for moderation, then it was very important to most of them that it be Ike's moderation, and for many it was not Ike's moderation for which they voted but just for Ike.

Why was Mr. Eisenhower so popular? Arthur Larson, the writer of a Republican book that Mr. Eisenhower liked, said it was because he had captured the middle position — the "Authentic American Center" — between the "extremes" of the past. He adhered to clear-cut, fundamental principles, said Mr. Larson, and developed a firm and consistent philosophy — a philosophy that almost all Americans can agree to (all but a few culls who may be lumped together as "the opposition"). But surely Mr. Larson claimed too little for his man, while claiming too much for his political philosophy.

Mr. Eisenhower had a middle ground appeal, to be sure. But it was a mistake to interpret even the middle ground as composed primarily of devotees of the position Mr. Larson expressed; many Americans were in the middle not because they had a definite political position but because they did not. In the first years of Mr. Eisenhower's popularity, these "middle-of-the-roader's" were plumping for Mr. Eisenhower without really knowing whether he was middle-of-the-road or not. They sought a man. It was the aboveness of that man and not just the middleness that created the Eisenhower phenomenon.

That major theme may have drowned out the others. One might even find a touch of pathos in Mr. Eisenhower's valiant but vain effort to make his principles catch up with his popularity. He made speeches expounding a dynamically conservative middle-of-the-road philosophy, but the applause regularly was greater when he was first introduced, before he said a single middle-of-the-road word, than after he had spoken. His untouchable aboveness not only outdistanced the popularity of his program and philosophy, it may even have impeded it.

The popularity of Mr. Eisenhower expressed the desire to avoid policies and ideas, to depend on a man, to get away from complexity that prevents the development of American political philosophies, including Mr. Eisenhower's own. It detached him from the unpopular Republicans, the disliked subordinates, and the unfortunate policies with which the Democrats tried vainly to connect him. But it detached him, too, from fellow candidates, from the programs, and the political philosophy with which the Republicans wanted to connect him.

Therefore, he was little help to other Republicans, or to his own political philosophy, and had little lasting impact on that party or position. He passed triumphantly through our political history, leaving our politics and his party pretty much as he found them.

The major theme was not that he stood at the center of our politics, but that he stood at the center of our culture; not that he stood in the middle of alternative policies, but that he stood at the heart of American habits and values. He represented what men in this culture, with these habits and values, have looked for: the good man above politics.

Mr. Eisenhower was that good man above politics, both negatively and positively. He represented not only a unique attachment to the common virtues and values that are easy to recognize and that unify the people but also a unique detachment from the positions on social and political philosophy that are difficult to understand and that divide the people.

The negative aspect — being separated from all factional quarrels, policies, even politics itself — was as important as the positive. Mr. Eisenhower's military role enabled him to pursue a career that brought him into the public eye but permitted him to stay apart from the controversies of public affairs all through the turbulent days of the New Deal, the Second World War, and the cold war. This nonpolitical role meant that as a Republican candidate he could cut deeply into normally Democratic voting strength. It was helpful to him also because this nonpolitical tradition is a sturdy American heritage in its own right.

"Politics" is suspect as a realm of conflict to a people who believe harmony to be natural and easy, and as a realm of failure (the diplomats lose the peace after the soldiers win the wars), to a people who believe that anything can be done by an enthusiastic decision of the will, and as a realm of compromise with evil, to a people whose heritage it has been to begin with unsullied moral ideals. Mr. Eisenhower could be presented as the negation of all that is meant by politics — a symbol of the simplicity, success, unity, and idealism of the American people as a whole.

His own life and behavior ideally conditioned him to this role. No one knew what party he belonged to; even after becoming a politician he frequently and no doubt truthfully said, "I'm no politician."

He was seen to be better and higher than all that. He represented all the aboveness one could want: personality, Americanism, spiritual values, and moral crusades — all "above politics."

The public saw Mr. Eisenhower not first of all as the representative of a party or of policy but as a man, an individual, a "personality." In an age when "personality" is something one may "have," Mr. Eisenhower was one of those who had it in great quantities. He was perceived as a warm, sincere, likable man, a man with that gift of open, unpretentious, relaxed, informal friendliness which is a feature of the American West at its best, a man from — the perfect place — Abilene, with a grin, who leaves the great international meeting to shop for a doll for his granddaughter, who greeted his troops by saying "My name's Eisenhower," who is an ordinary recognizable human being whom people "like."

One common interpretation made of Mr. Eisenhower a "father image." But he did not represent one part of the paternal pattern, the element of authority, resistance, reprimand, restraint. Mr. Eisenhower was not a father who was expected to demand much of his children. He was not the man who pounds his desk to show that he is boss; he had a well-known ability to make people get along together and to form a team, and a well-known desire to be liked. His political activity was not marked by vigorous leadership. If Mr. Eisenhower was indeed a father to Americans, he was the very American father of a democratic progressive family.

There is no doubt that this personality was sincere. The signs by which a public judges sincerity appear to include a visible fervor and earnestness of manner; a set of plain, familiar, and uncomplicated sentiments; and a constant willingness to make one's ideas completely explicit. One of the characteristics of a popular democracy may be its tendency to take things at face value; as publics become larger, the ability to see beneath the surface becomes smaller; what a man repeatedly says is what he is; what he doesn't say, he is not.

Mr. Eisenhower had the ability to make very explicit his patriotic, moral, and religious feelings; he could *say* the words repeatedly and with simple fervor.

Kevin McCann reports that he said, in the period before he became a political figure, "All I do is belabor the obvious." But the belaboring of the obvious may be exactly the right stance for a successful public figure in American democracy. The genius of Mr. Eisenhower's political personality may have been his gift for speaking platitudes sincerely.

But it would be a mistake to conclude from all this, from the slogan "I Like Ike," from the nationally televised and sentimental birthday parties, from the celebration of Mamie, the grin, and the President's sincerity, that personality in this sense was the sole source of his appeal. Part of it was the image of personality, sincerity, and warmth, but another part was the image of leadership, ability, and accomplishment.

This aspect of his public image was established supremely and beyond cavil by his military career. He was the great leader in an enterprise in which, unlike in any factional struggle, nearly all Americans shared; an enterprise which, unlike any in art or legislation or scholarship, had ends that were immediately understandable to every citizen. The leader in North Africa, the commander of Overlord, the agent of D-Day, the chief of NATO needed no further demonstration to fix in the public mind, firmly and forever, his strength, his skill, his decisiveness, his leadership. Perhaps, after he had fulfilled these roles, his strength was established whether thereafter he was strong or not; his decisiveness became unquestionable whether he took decisions or not; and his leadership was obvious whether he led or not.

Mr. Eisenhower was not at all a "man on horseback," not a "beloved leader" in the tradition of military heroes. He was personable, warm, and democratic at the same time that he was practical, strong, and able. In Eisenhower's case, the fame, the reputation for national leadership, and the passionate support engendered in war were immensely heightened by his friendly and democratic personal bearing. Richard Rovere wrote: "Eisenhower, with nothing to give them but his smile, made a neat and unpretentious appearance before the high and mighty of Europe in the kind of jacket worn here at home by fastidious gas station attendants . . ."

Since his personality was a standard American type, he might be said narrowly to have escaped being a colorless figure; without his career, he would not have been a person of particular interest. But, given his superlative career, his ordinariness became a virtue: the victor in history's mightiest battles was a nice guy too. He had none of the qualities that the ordinary man finds annoying, and refuses to acknowledge, because they are outside his experience and imply some claim for deference. Mr. Eisenhower combined the perennial grandeur of success in battle with the familiar friendliness of the man next door.

His appeal as President was separate from any concrete achievement. He was the static symbol of long-accepted virtues and the embodiment of perennial suprapolitical values. He was not only a good man; he was a man whose goodness does not

need to be proved. A feature of the Eisenhower phenomenon
was the predisposition of the American to believe the best of
Mr. Eisenhower. The American blamed subordinates but not
the President; he doubted others but trusted Mr. Eisenhower.
The farmer might blame Mr. Benson, the workingman Mr.
Wilson or Mr. Weeks, the Southerner Richard Nixon or Earl
Warren. The voter might reject the Republican Party, the
Administration's policies, and the new conservatism but still
like Ike — and not only like him but vote for him.

Mr. Eisenhower's goodness was axiomatic, taken for granted,
and taken as sufficient for all things; by it, men and policies
could be measured, tested, defended. Mr. Eisenhower himself
often seemed to be a believer in this part, as in other aspects, of
his own myth: when challenged, criticized, or disagreed with,
he would often cite the goodness of his own intentions.

Mr. Eisenhower also was a perfect repository for the bipartisan or suprapartisan national piety that surrounds the
Presidential office at any time, and that was particularly strong
in the 1950's — the soft nationalism that knows there is a
domain of the common and good and American that is more
important than all the "things that divide us."

Any candidate of the more conservative party, reflecting the
harmonistic outlook of the established groups in society, will
tend to speak calming words of unity and harmony against
what people of that stripe regard as the divisive and con-
tentious attitude of their opponents. Governor Dewey built
his campaign in 1948 almost entirely around this theme, and it
was certainly one note in Mr. Eisenhower's campaigns; to
some of his followers he did represent the unity and harmony
of the country as a whole, after years of Democratic emphasis

on class strife and division. But his attraction on this point cut much deeper than would that of an ordinary conservative's recommendation that we all work together, that nobody rock the boat or be a knocker, and that we all remember what a great country we have here — even though Mr. Eisenhower himself was a prime source of material in that general line. When *he* spoke that way he did so as a hero of a great national effort, and as a man transparently free from any awareness of the ideological significance of what he was saying. And he did so also as a man who himself embodied, almost to perfection, a popular pattern of Americanism. Put Mr. Eisenhower's public personality alongside any description of what is typically American: they correspond exactly. Items from books on American traits, and from Eisenhower biographies are perfectly interchangeable.

We may say that archetypal Americanism as described by observers from abroad, or by social scientists, or by anyone else, is made up of two elements: the practical, competitive, individualistic, externally minded, environment-mastering, and success-seeking on the one side, and the "spiritual," idealistic, friendly, team-working, moralizing, and reform-seeking on the other. Mr. Eisenhower exactly summarized both.

The treatises on what is typically American always point to our seeking of success and our emphasis upon achievement, in the most tangible, worldly terms; to our practicality and pragmatism; to our opposition to theory, contemplation, and speculation; to our optimism about what a man can do, and our energy in doing it; to a whole bias toward a direct, external, practical, productive relation to the world. Mr. Eisenhower fits that exactly. The text of his own remarks, indeed, often sounds like a broad parody of the local spokesman for Americanism, or like an effort to capture the type made by some bad

novelist of mildly un-American leanings: "My friend, the Defense Department is spending something like forty billion dollars a year of our money . . . Who would you rather have in
charge of that, some failure that never did anything, or a successful businessman? I got the head of the biggest company I
could go to, General Motors, and said, 'Will you come in and
do this for us?' "

His own career represented the "success" that he, like the
standard American, admired: he went from Abilene to unassailable world fame. In a society attuned to tangible accomplishment, Mr. Eisenhower was a supreme success in the most
obviously and unchallengeably practical of all activities, the
defense of the nation itself.

Mr. Eisenhower's education and intellectual bent were consistently described in the practical, American terms in sympathetic biographies written well before he became a presidential candidate — during and after the war. John Gunther said:
"His main mental characteristic is drive. He is practical
minded; he hates what he calls 'forensics'; theory irritates him
and he believes in first things first." * Kenneth Davis wrote:
"Externalism was the order of the day and it suited him . . .
Only the physical was 'really real'; the mind was but the tool of
the body; ideas were valid only in so far as they were scenes
for immediate practical action." †

As young Dwight Eisenhower was about to enter a new
school, Mr. Davis summarized his early world: "The new
possibilities, like the old, were physical, spatial, stimulating to
action rather than thought, to the practical body rather than
the contemplative mind . . . His world, enlarged, continued

---

* *Eisenhower: The Man and Symbol* (New York: Harper, 1951), page 24.
† Kenneth Davis' book, still the best one about Mr. Eisenhower, is *Eisenhower: Soldier of Democracy* (New York: Doubleday, 1945). This and the
following quotations come from pages 76, 71, 73, 73, 117, 370–371.

indifferent if not hostile to inward brooding and abstract speculation. It was a world of, by and for the extroverted."

In school: ". . . His mind had no natural bent toward
generalized speculation, where terms are altogether abstract
and symbolic, but . . . he dealt easily and effectively with
subjects in which the terms are objective and concrete."

In the study of history: "He was not encouraged by either
teacher or environment to shape in his mind even the most
rudimentary philosophy of history. His interests were all
pragmatic and particular."

"He had no desire to be known as a 'bone file,' a 'bookworm,'
a 'grind,' " Mr. Davis wrote. "He was far more interested in
becoming a football star."

Davis had occasion to discuss Eisenhower's education in
politics, after the description of his part in the North African
political troubles of World War II:

> His was, as we have seen, a remarkably "unpolitical" educa-
> tion, from a Kansas village through West Point into the Army.
> It is true that he had read a great deal of history, but he had
> concentrated on military history, and his attention had been
> confined primarily to events and personalities . . . it seems evi-
> dent that he had relatively little conception of history as trend
> or process . . . Consequently he was perhaps too inclined to
> underrate the importance of principles, of ideologies, as deter-
> mining forces in history . . . one might say that here the
> frontier pragmatism which has so largely determined the char-
> acter of modern American education revealed, through Eisen-
> hower, certain basic weaknesses . . .

American optimism, too, the conviction that "the impossible
takes a little longer," was not missing: "Basically . . . Eisenhower is an optimistic person. 'I've never heard him say that
something couldn't be done,' recalls one aide. Eisenhower

rarely misses an opportunity to try to infect those around him with this 'nothing is impossible' feeling." *

Most of all, he represented a classical American individualism. He represented it in obvious ways: in his constant reduction of vast questions of social policy to the understandable dimensions of his "respect" for one or another person, in his innocence about the way ideas cluster ideologically around the interests of social groups.

But he also represented American individualism in another way, a way that goes to the heart of American attitudes toward politics: he reflected the position that the main thing is the motive and character of individuals, rather than the forms of politics; that real human progress must come about by the changing hearts of individuals more than by changes in the arrangements of society. "Now, I have consistently tried over five and a half years to show," Mr. Eisenhower said, typically, in a press conference comment dealing with racial issues, ". . . that mere law will never solve this problem. I believe we have got to look inside ourselves . . ."

A trust in the inward change of heart or will, with an accompanying emphasis on exhortation, is a characteristic of this country's outlook. Beginning with the picture of the unencumbered individual, affected only secondarily by his social surroundings, then proceeding to a great trust in this individual's heart and will and fundamental goodness, this outlook places great store in persuasion, and on verbal declarations of intentions and resolutions of purpose.

Conflicts and difficulties, if unfortunately they do arise, are seen to flow from the evil will of a few individuals, not from kinks in the social arrangements. This view overlooks the less

* This quotation is from *The Revolt of the Moderates* by Samuel Lubell (New York: Harper, 1955), page 33.

visible forms of power (market control, mass manipulation, power of position, "mere law") and does not see the continuous, inescapable, and pervasive place of power in social life. It relies heavily, therefore, on appeals to good will. Those who hold to it deal in hortatory and declaratory politics; in Eisenhower Doctrines, Declarations of Washington, and Baghdad Pacts; in combating a depression by telling consumers that they "auto buy now." When the voluntary means break down, however, this way of thinking can swiftly show quite another side. It can turn suddenly from hortatory appeals to good will to angry use of force: from Newport's meeting to Little Rock's troops, from the good-will tour to the dispatch of Marines. Because the picture of the world has been — too much — that of a scatter of individuals, only secondarily and voluntarily related to each other, the American holder of these views does not have a sufficiently graduated and subtle view of power.

The other large complex of American values has to do with idealism and reform, with morality and religion. The most untouchable element of Mr. Eisenhower's "aboveness," and one of the most exasperating to some of his opponents, was his identification with the generalized religious interest that was widespread during his Presidency.

Mr. Stanley High, a one-time speech writer for Mr. Eisenhower, wrote in *The Reader's Digest* in the spring after the first victory that a "revival of moral and spiritual faith in America" is "what Eisenhower really wants." "He believes that religion and the 'godly virtues' account for America's beginning and its growth . . . He believes that, save in a renewal of that faith and those virtues, there is no answer for the future . . ." * One suspected at the time that the ghost-

---

* Mr. High's article appeared in *The Reader's Digest*, April 1953.

writer might be doing a little ghost-thinking — that Mr. High, a *Digest* specialist in things moral and spiritual, and a former writer of "inspirational messages" for Franklin Roosevelt, might himself have been a source for some of the material he used to show President Eisenhower's feelings. There might be a difference, one thought, between what Eisenhower really wanted and what an Eisenhower speech writer really wanted Eisenhower to want. But the years showed that Mr. High was indeed on Mr. Eisenhower's wavelength on this point, and that a large American public was, too.

The Reverend Edward L. R. Elson, the pastor of the Washington church of which Mr. Eisenhower was a member, wrote an ecstatic book later on about the religious mission of his most famous parishioner: "It may not be too much to say that through his personal conduct and expression he has become the focal point of a moral resurgence and spiritual awakening of national proportions." * Witnesses less involved personally in moral resurgences and spiritual awakenings than Mr. Elson and Mr. High granted, at least, that Mr. Eisenhower spoke often of those subjects.

"This crusade is soundly based on moral and spiritual values," said Mr. Eisenhower. "Faith in God and country; that's Eisenhower — how about you?" said billboards in California.

Mr. Eisenhower voiced exactly the standard themes of the popular "revival" that took place during his period in office: the belief in "believing" or in "faith," independent of its object ("These devoted people meeting here," he said to the World Council of Churches at Evanston, "believe, first of all, always in faith . . ."); the emphasis on feeling rather than on content or meaning ("a *deeply felt* religion"); the recommendation of

---

* Mr. Elson's book is *America's Spiritual Recovery* (New Jersey: Revell, 1954). The quotation is from page 48.

religion for its usefulness ("faith is the mightiest force that man has at his command"); the connection of this generalized religion with America's "foundation," as he said over and over again; and finally, the differentiation of America from the Communist world chiefly on the basis of this "religious" view.

Criticism of all this appeared to him to be too subtle, too verbal, too "intellectual." After all, he seemed to say, we all know what we are trying to say here. Through Mr. Eisenhower's remarks ran a small note of impatience at the sophisticated niceties of, as he called them in the 1956 campaign, "those who dwell with words and phrases." "We believe," he said proudly to a gathering of Republicans in 1953, "that our thinking and our emotions are unclouded by the various brands of cynicism that bear the label of political sophistication." And of the subject at hand, he said on another occasion, "Faith seems to be too simple a thing for some people to understand."

There was an evident connection in Mr. Eisenhower's mind between his expression of faith and his role as President. Milton Eisenhower, asked by Bela Kornitzer about the "change" in his brother's attitude toward religious ritual when he became President, gave this reply:

> I think he may not like the purely ritualistic aspects of religion because they are merely an outward manifestation, whereas the true significance of religion is something that is in the mind and in the heart . . . Now, when you become the leader of a free world, it becomes necessary not only to find the inner satisfaction which religious understanding can bring, but also to stimulate others in a thousand ways. Well, here we come to another fact, then: Ours is a religious nation. . . . all of our basic documents are political expressions of certain cardinal religious concepts. Thus, it is necessary, I think, in order to protect American democracy and freedom in the world, for the President of the United States to give spiritual stimulation . . .

Most people find it best to adhere to religious conviction through some physical connection with the church and physical participation in ritualistic exercises. This being so, it is good and right for the President of the United States to go to church regularly . . .*

For Mr. Eisenhower himself, an "inner" expression without "ritual" was perhaps sufficient; but for the President of the United States, in order to protect American democracy a "physical connection" was required. As another brother, Edgar, said while discussing the same question, "He is the representative of the American people. As their representative he must set an example in his conduct."

Mr. Eisenhower also set an example in regard to the inseparable companion to "spiritual values" in those years, namely "moral values." "Ladies and gentlemen, you have summoned me," he said, right away on accepting his first presidential nomination, ". . . to lead a great crusade . . ." The word "crusade" appeared three more times in the next few sentences of his acceptance speech at the Republican convention; and crusades for this and crusades for that crisscrossed the country in the years thereafter at a rate that must have been greater than the Holy Land ever knew, even in its busiest season.

Actually Mr. Eisenhower in office was something rather different from a crusader. His characteristic merits, for his supporters, were those of meditation, conciliation, pacification; his characteristic faults, for his critics, were those of the "green fairways of complacency." The Eisenhower "moral crusade" really was one of the tamest and gentlest of political movements. What was the cause? Who was the infidel, where the

---

* Bela Kornitzer, *The Great American Heritage* (New York: Farrar, Strauss, and Cudahy, 1955), page 137.

Holy City? The first evil against which the crusade was directed was "the mess in Washington"; presumably that battle was won very early, but the crusade went on.

This amorphous quality may be a product of the debilitating effect that the black arts of public relations and advertising have on words, particularly popular and/or honorable words like "faith," "sincerity," "righteousness," and "morality." The appropriateness of the "crusade" idea to the public in our time, like the use of "sincerity" in the advertising fraternity, may show a desire to recapture a virtue now lost and nostalgically remembered — in the case of the crusade, a moral zeal and purpose attributed to generations past.

But wizardry does not entirely account for the "crusade." Something was really there, intrinsic to the mind of large numbers of his supporters: an inclination to see the world divided into simple moral alternatives and to assume that by rousing energy one can eliminate the evil.

The "moral" tone sounded throughout the Eisenhower Administration. A so-called "moral issue" was, in fact, the key to the victory with which the Eisenhower period began: the victory over the supporters of Senator Taft within the Republican Party.

A study by political scientists of the battle among Republicans in 1952 says "probably no single factor in the entire preconvention struggle had a greater bearing on the outcome than the Texas controversy," * and nothing had greater bearing on that controversy than the Eisenhower faction's casting it in "moral" terms about which one could be absolute, and hence win an unmitigated victory.

At Mineral Wells, Texas, on May 27, 1952, the Taft forces

* Paul T. David, et al., *Presidential Nominating Politics in 1952: The National Story* (Baltimore: Johns Hopkins Press, 1954). Quotations are from pages 50, 53, 91, and 53.

were able to control the state Republican convention, and prevent the seating of the Eisenhower delegates. These latter then withdrew to a rump convention, and nominated an alternative slate of delegates for Texas' thirty-eight votes in the Republican national convention. These two separate slates of delegates continued to contest the seats until the struggle was resolved on the third day of the national convention. But meanwhile the question was projected into the national scene, where the Taft and Eisenhower forces were embattled, as a "steal," and it received remarkable nationwide publicity in a press which the Taft forces charged with favoritism to Eisenhower.

Summarizing the Eisenhower faction's struggle against the Taft group, the study says: "Eisenhower, with fewer committed delegates, needed an issue . . . In Ike's case, the issue of the Texas 'steal' seemed heaven-sent. His managers made the most of it, for they kept beating their tom-toms until the Taft leaders finally yielded completely."

Mr. Eisenhower himself responded to the case as it was presented to him with righteous indignation. Something *immoral* had happened, and that made the political struggle, otherwise complex, become clear. "His fighting blood had been aroused," said Merlo Pusey. "He was ready to roar across the country for clean and decent operations . . . he would fight 'to keep our party clean and fit to lead our nation!' . . . it was he who decided to fight on aspects of the 'Texas issue' because he regarded it as a question of principle . . . the struggle within the party was a 'straight out issue of right and wrong.'" *

It is notable how regularly issues of "straight out right and wrong" arose in Mr. Eisenhower's political career, beginning at its very start. He was "moral" not only against Stevenson and

* *Eisenhower The President* (New York: Macmillan, 1956), page 210.

Truman, but against Taft. This may suggest not only that there is a large supply of immorality around in the world, for those who want to condemn it, but also that Mr. Eisenhower is a man who looks for this kind of clear, black and white, "moral" definition of the environment.

Of the actual merits of the case, the political scientists' study says, "there was little reason to consider either state convention *wholly* representative of Texas Republicans."

The "corruption" issue, of course, helped to bring to birth the "moral" theme in the Eisenhower movement; it was a line of attack with obvious sterling qualities for the Republican Party. It helped to provide that "cause" that the Republicans needed. The Republican attempt to regain a majority has involved the effort to find ways to erase the memories of the depression and the thirties, and to supplant economic and welfare issues with other issues. "Communism" and "Korea" helped to fill the need, but "corruption" provided the most unanswerable issue of all. The moral crusade arose, in part, as a Republican negative on that conveniently onesided issue.

But, corruption was also the sort of issue that many leaders and followers of the Eisenhower movement themselves could respond to anyway: it was clear, it was simple, it was moral; it did evoke social passion, but it did not involve social change. This problem was not lost in a maze of impersonal, social forces, but was the plain result of the work of bad men, of a different sort and separate from the crusaders.

Richard Hofstader, writing about another expression of American morality in politics, the "progressive impulse" of the early part of the century, said:

> . . . the middle class citizen received quite earnestly the exhortations that charged him with personal responsibility for all kinds of social ills. It was his business to do something about

them . . . But what would he do? He was too substantial a
fellow to want to make any basic changes in a society in which
he was typically a prosperous and respectable figure. What he
needed, therefore, was a *feeling* that action was taking place, a
sense that the moral tone of things was being improved and
that he had a part in this improvement. Corruption was thus
become a particularly fine issue for the moral energies of the
Progressive.*

The Progressive Mr. Hofstader describes seems similar to the
moral crusader of Mr. Eisenhower's time.

But the "moral" cast to the Eisenhower movement went beyond the issues like corruption on which an individualistic
and a social ethic join; it went beyond the campaign period,
with its indictment of the "moral tone" of the preceding administration, into the speech and thought of the new administration.

When Mr. Eisenhower made his second acceptance speech,
to the Republican convention in San Francisco in the summer
of 1956, for example, he made it very clear that he preferred
principle to expediency. He was accepting his party's nomination for a second term as President of the United States, and
he set his own philosophy — the philosophy that had guided
his first administration — in direct opposition to that of a recent, unnamed previous President, whose identity (and party)
most of his hearers probably could guess. "One of my prede-
cessors," noted President Eisenhower, "is said to have observed
that in making his decisions he had to operate like a football
quarterback — he could not very well call the next play until
he saw how the last play had turned out. Well, that may be
a good way to run a football team, but in these times it is no
way to run a government." Mr. Eisenhower insisted, instead,

* *The Age of Reform* (New York: Knopf, 1955), page 210.

that "great government programs be based upon principle rather than upon shifting political opportunism"; he said that "without solid guidelines of enduring principle, national policies flounder in confusion"; and then he gave "several examples of rejecting expediency in favor of principle." Each example set what "Principle" says in direct opposition to what "Expediency" says. The three examples were "the farm issue" ("for this man of principle, the farmer, we have designed our program of principle"), "labor relations" and "concentration of power in Washington." The use of a frame like the Principle-Expediency one is standard speech-writing practice, of course, and so is the stark contrast between one party's view and the other's. But the Eisenhower administration was even more prone than the ordinary run of political movements to speak that way. This "morality" deals not with a complicated field of contending values but with simple, abstract, absolute rules. Mr. Eisenhower regularly and proudly referred to his principles as "fixed" and "firm" (as he did, for example, in both inaugural addresses). Discussing our action in the tangle of the Suez crisis, Mr. Eisenhower said: "There are some firm principles that cannot bend — they can only break. And we shall not break ours." A declaration like that has such a noble ring in general that it is hard to make clear the defects of its application in the particular case. As with Mr. Eisenhower himself, it is protected from moral condemnation of results by the transparent goodness of intentions.

The Eisenhower campaigns established a feeling among many that the appeals to the lower instincts (the pocketbook) were made by the Democrats, while the appeals to the higher motivations and larger possibilities were made by Mr. Eisenhower, and that voting for him was noble, right, responsible and good.

The heart of the conception of the Eisenhower movement was that it was something more than ordinary politics; this campaign sprang from motives higher than those of political and economic interest; this "crusade" attacked an evil which — though vague — was more serious than mere disagreement over political policy; this candidate was in touch with principles higher than those known to ordinary politicians.

As the crusaders saw it, moral considerations were something separate from and above mere political considerations, and their movement partook of this different and higher order: "He's not in this just as a politician. He's in this for moral reasons."

The crusade struck the deep public desire for a way around the complexities of political decision. The voters knew there were all those complex policy problems. But candidate Eisenhower was working at a different level, a higher level. His was not a campaign to get something for his followers, but a crusade, a noble effort to do what is good. It was *moral* not political. It is hard to decide about political campaigns, but to a moral crusade the answer can be clear and pure.

Americans want to combine their large themes without contradiction: to be both practical and idealistic, successful and moral, rich yet overflowing with spiritual values. Mr. Eisenhower expressed the practical and success-seeking aspect of American society at the time of its greatest opulence; and he represented also the simplest and oldest version of a "moral" heritage, at the time of obvious danger from an opposing power. He represented both and he represented them in combination rather than in contradiction, in mutual support rather than in tension. He combined these strands exactly as popular American ideas want to combine them. An Eisenhower enthusiast like Merlo J. Pusey, for example, would follow a paragraph about the President's ideals with a prompt reminder that

he keeps them within the budget: "He lifts men to higher aims
and greater devotion. Without any assumption of self-righteousness, he focuses the public mind upon constructive ideas
and Christian virtues . . . Yet his idealism has been kept
within practical bounds. While sponsoring foreign-aid programs costing the taxpayers billions of dollars each year, he
had not overlooked the necessity of keeping our own economy
sound."

The anti-political element in each set of American characteristics is redoubled when they are thus neatly reconciled to
each other, all tension removed. Mr. Eisenhower's "aboveness"
was the quintessence of this redoubled American rejection of
politics. He united its two sources. The practical strand tends
to sink below the problems of policy and value in politics down
into the domain of technique and administration, solving everything by "know-how," a good staff system, one-page summaries,
clean desks, "best brains," and business-in-government. The
moralistic strand is inclined to soar above the conflicts and
concrete decisions of politics into the cloudless realms of
"moral and spiritual values"; and to step aside into a realm of
inner and individual "righteousness."

The last years of the Eisenhower administration did not
have the euphoric aspect that some felt in its middle years.
After the Korean war ended, and Stalin died, and Senator Mc-
Carthy was eclipsed, there was a summit of the Eisenhower
mood, along about 1955: Ike was in his White House and all
was right with the world. There was a moment when a broad
and popular America saw its own ideal image realized. But
in the later 1950's things changed: if not with the Hungarian
revolution and Suez crisis of 1956, then certainly with Sputnik
in 1957, and with the events of Little Rock, the recession of

1958, the Berlin crisis of 1958 and following, the U–2 and abortive summit of 1959, the riots in Japan. Mr. Eisenhower, of course, remained popular, but reporters noticed a certain public reticence about him. "Aboveness" had not altogether worked out. The persisting American illusion that there can be an escape from politics had received a blow. Perhaps it was about to die, but it would be a painful death.

Notes on a Moral Crusade

1. THE CORRUPTION OF CORRUPTION

1952

In 1950–52 the United States of America suddenly had an attack of "lower moral standards." "Mink coat — deep freeze — Washington" became a familiar syndrome. Politicians dared to hope that in the mink coats they had at last something for which they had been looking in vain for twenty years. Preachers thought that here at last in the maze of politics was a Clear Moral Issue upon which they could speak loudly and forthrightly, because it was so very, very Moral.

The evidence was provided by congressional investigations of the RFC, the Bureau of Internal Revenue, and "crime"; and by tabloid sensations about point-shaving by basketball teams and favors to athletes at West Point. It made a heady mixture, especially if you threw in a dash of the divorce rate and drunkenness.

The talk of "mess" and "corruption" allows us to give way to that belief, always perversely attractive to humankind, that now things are *really* going to the dogs. The modern world is complicated and frustrating. Our need to express our emotions about it far outruns our ability to comprehend it. We don't want a balanced analysis — you can't get mad at a graph. We want a villain to punch in the nose, and one of the chief needs Washington fills is to parade these villains.

We want the evil-doers to be persons different and separate from us, with whom we need feel no identification. The villain in the movies, when the code allowed it, was a foreigner of some sort; the "politicians" and "bureaucrats" of our popular mythology of government are a different breed from the rest of us. A group of Republicans from Texas, in New York for an Eisenhower rally, sang a song beginning:

> *Deep freeze and minks, and all*
> *those pinks,*
> *You bet they're not from Texas . . .*

Strange patterns of association appear. Truman was somehow responsible for the weakness of college basketball players, and the peculations of a county sheriff in Florida were said to show the "corruption" of the administration in Washington.

One notable thing about the hullabaloo over "corruption" is the marked contrast between the size and seriousness of the publicity, and the size and seriousness of the remedies. The Kefauver television crime show engaged the transfixed attention of the whole nation, but what became of it all, except an increase in public despair?

The chief reasons for "corruption" are the fast and confusing growth of government, which has meant that the financial capital has shifted to Washington; the fragmented political organizations; and the absence of an accepted standard of public service. The direction of an enormous government falls into the hands of random individuals who are elected on the basis of personal ties and local favors.

Individuals in various pockets of power must be dealt with, and administrative officials find that the private group constituency is more powerful and more helpful than party leadership, and so they become friends of the private group and agents to the government.

Behind the defects stands no evil demon, but ourselves. The defects in party responsibility and administrative morale and standards are the result of the public's own attitude toward politics.

The officials we choose, and the private persons who bribe them, come out of a public whose attitude toward government they share.

If that attitude is cynical, then the corrupt results should not surprise us and no mere change of party will alter them.

What do we expect of politics and government? If this is seen as a dark, dirty, unpleasant maze of restriction, to be tolerated grudgingly, and regarded cynically, then the attitude of government officials and of private groups toward government will be cynical and exploitative, negative and attentive to private advantage, like our own.

The paradox is this: that the sweeping and extreme cry of "corruption" springs out of and adds to that cynical attitude toward government which produces "corruption."

2. EISENHOWER, MORALIST

July 7, 1953

As a candidate Mr. Eisenhower went well beyond the moral attack on the "corruption" of the Truman regime that might have been expected of any Republican, and as a President he has gone well beyond the standard obeisances to God of a public figure as he approaches the end of his speech.

Although he won votes with it, Mr. Eisenhower plainly did not employ the "God stuff," as Franklin Roosevelt is reported to have called it, simply as a political device. His sincerity was part of his appeal.

The President's constant "moral" language may be partly a

substitute for a developed social philosophy. It is at any rate a bit sudden. Mr. Eisenhower did not seem to be especially concerned with "moral and spiritual" matters during his Army career.

But when he first spoke as a politician in Abilene in June, 1952, he insisted that our most important strength is "spiritual values," and he kept it up all through his campaign. It was an approach to politics that the audience understood and liked, religious without being divisive, moral without being unpleasant. Like Ike, Americans remember with reverence a pious heritage, the form and spirit but not the content of which they want to preserve.

Mr. Eisenhower's special emphasis on the moral and spiritual coincides with his participation in politics, perhaps because this new role demands something new of him. He is an expert at choosing and effecting practical means to a determined objective. But in politics the choice is not only among means but among objectives.

He has the gift of bringing men to work together by touching the sources of friendliness and common purpose within them. He is able to do this because the big, clear differences, as between free men and totalitarians, are of primary importance to him, and he tends to relegate to a secondary place the more subtle differences that are the stuff of politics.

These characteristic abilities of Mr. Eisenhower may be nonpolitical, but they are very American. Therefore they are successful in American politics.

Mr. Eisenhower may have found clear lines of operation for politics by taking the American Constitution pretty much as it would be taught in a civics course. The branches of the government are three, and these are separate, and these "coordinate branches" each have proper spheres, not to be invaded by the others. It is even helpful to explain to God, in the inaugural prayer, that one is praying only for the Executive Branch.

In a way, what President Eisenhower appears to have done is to leap at once from the certainties of the practical world clear over the ambiguities of social philosophy into the certainties of absolute morality and religion. His campaign was explicitly shaped to convince the voters of his sincere morality rather than to explain to them a program that might be followed.

The certainty with which the "moral and spiritual values" are held is for Mr. Eisenhower an emotional rather than an intellectual certainty. The phrase which he constantly used is revealing: "a deeply felt religious faith." Depth of feeling is the important thing, rather than any objective meaning. One might say that President Eisenhower, like many Americans, is a very fervent believer in a very vague religion.

The General said over and over during the campaign that when the founding fathers said that men were endowed by their Creator with rights, they showed that the basis or foundation of this nation and form of government lay in a "deeply felt religious faith." Our government is the attempt to "translate" that religion into the political world. He said that no other nation has America's "spiritual and moral strength." He said that "the Almighty takes a definite and direct interest day by day in the progress of this nation." Religion appears as a wholesale endorsement of the aims and purposes of America, "the mightiest power which God has yet seen fit to put upon his footstool."

The values that spring from this commitment to religion-in-general are values-in-general. Once he named some of them this way, "Honesty, decency, fairness, service — all that sort of thing."

The most definite thing President Eisenhower said about values was that they are not material. He said, "What we are really trying to defend is a way of life, a scale of moral and spiritual values. You are not just trying to save your own pocketbook." He often implied that moral values and a spiritual (i.e., nonpocketbook) outlook were identical, and that his opponents were presenting a materialistic, and therefore immoral, program as against his spiritual, and therefore moral, one.

The contrast between mere politics and Eisenhower's moral crusade appeared throughout his speeches. What he was engaged in was not a mere political campaign of just another political candidate, but something else — a moral crusade.

From this center have come several corollary doctrines.

First, there is the doctrine of the hound's tooth. Since this is a moral crusade, the crusaders must be moral. But since morality is something different from politics, the "moral" cleanliness we ask about is simply personal, and has nothing to do with policy.

When Mr. Nixon was challenged about his fund, Mr. Eisenhower quite morally insisted he must be "clean." He convinced himself, perhaps with some help from audience reaction, that Nixon was personally "honest" and joined Mr. Nixon in calling the whole challenge a smear.

The challenge had not been against Mr. Nixon's honesty in dealing with public or private monies at all, but the crusaders answered in these terms alone. Thus the result of the moral crusade may be to dull rather than to awaken moral concern. The more subtle and probably more important moral questions like those involved in the Nixon Fund are excluded from consideration.

Second, there is the doctrine of the incorruptible man. Morality, which is personal hound's-tooth cleanliness, is absolutely distinguishable from immorality. There are the corrupt, who will be replaced "from top to bottom," and the "incorruptible men," who will replace them. These seem to be permanent and exclusive categories.

The moral crusade thus tends to regard the separation of moral from immoral as an absolute division between men, rather than a relative and shifting division between values and patterns which come mixed in varying proportions in particular men. This gives the moral crusade clarity, but it also gives it rigidity in dealing with the real world. It may also cause the crusaders to ignore the structural causes of persistent immoral situations.

Charles E. Wilson's remarkable attitude at the Senate hearings on his confirmation had the flavor of this doctrine. He seemed to be saying to the senators who had the effrontery to ask him questions about his holdings that, after all, corruption had been thrown out by definition when the Democrats were defeated and that he could not be considered susceptible to temptation. He was a member of the moral crusade.

Third, there is the doctrine of the blameless public.

One of the most interesting exchanges of the campaign was that between Mr. Stevenson's Los Angeles speech on corruption and Mr. Eisenhower's reply in Columbia, South Carolina. Governor Stevenson said that the morality of the public official could rise no higher than the morality of the public. He maintained that the final responsibility for corruption rested upon the public in general. General Eisenhower and his speech writers seized upon this with some glee, and worked it into the Columbia, South Carolina, speech. "Are you to blame for the loss of China?" he asked: "Are you to blame for this treadmill prosperity?" Or for the "Scandal-a-day administration"? The answer in each case was no.

Mr. Eisenhower was encouraging the American public's belief that an individual must bear the whole guilt for social evil, with the public bearing no share of responsibility.

The election after twenty years of a Republican prompts a comparison between the moral claims of the first and the current representatives of that party. Lincoln, too, was preoccupied with the moral implications of his acts. He saw the questions of slavery and union as moral questions. But he did not regard morality as an airtight category above and apart from the operation of politics. He, who had the clearest provocation to invoke the symbols of a righteous moral crusade, did not.

Lincoln did not imply that those who differed from him were not "moral." He explicitly stated at Cooper Union that the difference was one of sincere moral convictions on both sides. The absolutes of religion and morality were not identical with his side but above both sides, judging both. He prayed not that God be on his side but that he be on God's, and he left it to history to decide what was the moral crusade.

3. AN UNSPECIFIC DISCUSSION, NOT DEALING IN PERSONALITIES

June 8, 1954

A certain President — I do not give his name, since I do not deal in personalities — imposed on himself the rule not "to indulge in any kind of personalities under any pretext whatever."

The rule seemed plainly to have been formulated for the most worthy of motives: He did not want to add to the personal attacks that occur too often in politics. If others went ahead and engaged in name calling, at least he could refuse to join in it.

Unfortunately, the results of moral rules are not always as worthy as the motives for adopting them. Many voted for the President because they thought he would restrain his party; instead he restrained himself from restraining his party. And one form of this restraint was this rule against dealing with specific cases and persons.

The chief beneficiary of the "no personalities" rule was not a member of the Opposition but a member of this President's own party about whom the specific naming of a name was most important: a certain Senator. The President's rule resulted in remarkably roundabout and secondhand ways of resisting the increasingly aggressive acts of this Senator when the President resisted them at all — praise for a General whom the Senator had insulted; a TV commentator who had criticized the Senator was pronounced a friend (with no comment on the Senator's countercharges against the man's loyalty); a letter was sent to clergymen condemning sweeping attacks (not mentioning upon whom); and the Secretary of State was supported (without any mention of those who had accused the Secretary of sending "perfumed notes").

This roundaboutness left room for different interpretations. To friends of the President who opposed his senatorial adversary the meaning was obvious: "See? The President has spoken plainly against the Senator." But to real or potential friends of the Senator, who did not read the same newspapers, the meaning was not so obvious. And the Senator himself was all innocence. Book burning? Shucks, he can't mean me. I never burned any books. And the President, asked what he had meant, said — you guessed it — that he didn't deal in personalities.

The Senator and his cohorts were tough: for them forbearance meant retreat. Each foray that was not effectively resisted gave them still more audacity for the next, and by their very audacity they gained a still stronger position and had to be placated at a point marked by some greater excess.

The President regularly spoke up for Fair Play, Justice, and Decency. But everybody was for Fair Play, Justice, and Decency in general. The Senator did not endorse unfair play, injustice, and indecency, and thus join the issue. The question was not whether or not we should have fair play, etc., in general, but rather what, in specific cases, *was* fair play. In the absence of clear, specific, respected judgments to the contrary, a large section of the public took the Senator's word.

The President, in a TV chat intended to allay the country's fears, paid glowing tribute to the ability of American "public opinion" to prevent the Senator's abuses of congressional investigations. But this "public opinion" didn't grow in a void. It was dependent upon sources of fact and judgment. There was something odd in this most powerful of "opinion leaders" speaking and acting as though "public opinion" were a kind of independent magic force not subject to the leadership of people like himself. His default left a vacuum to be filled by more aggressive leaders of opinion, including the Senator.

One of the troubles with neat moral rules is that they may tend to limit rather than to expand a man's responsibility. A man feels he has done his part, and that any further responsibility rests with someone else — say with the Senate itself, or the people who elected the Senators. Or maybe the no-personalities rule relieves one of the necessity for making specific judgments in controversial matters even in one's private conscience.

But there seems to be something wrong at the very heart of that rule. Is it really impossible to declare oneself about acts of a specific politician without "indulging in personali-

ties"? To name a public figure and specifically to disagree
with him is not necessarily to attack him personally. One can
say a man is wrong in this policy or that action or in the whole
drift of his social philosophy, and still not be "dealing in personalities." If one adds that the man is obnoxious, dishonest,
a louse, a coward, and monumentally stupid, then that might
be dealing in personalities. But there is an important difference, and this President's rule did not allow for that difference. It left no room for a specific disagreement over policy.

The President, with his self-restraint, was almost the direct
opposite of the Senator as a type of political figure. But maybe
both reflected, in opposite ways, the same mistaken view of
politics. That view, unfortunately all too prevalent, tended to
squeeze out the area in which it was possible just to have dis-
agreements over policy. It made political questions subject to
absolute answers.

The Senator was notorious for this: A different position on
Far Eastern policy was not just wrong, it was treason; anyone
accused of having delayed the decision on the H-bomb had to
be a Communist. Opposition to the Senator's activities was
subversion; his fight was "the fight for America," which didn't
leave opponents much room.

The President's rule tended to suggest a polite form of this
same error by erasing the line between policy differences and
ultimate personal opposition. Admittedly this line was often
hard to locate, but the knowledge that it was there was crucial
to democracy. It made possible the continually shifting align-
ments of those who now agreed, now disagreed within a larger
framework of agreement and personal respect. Without it,
every political disagreement tended to become complete and
personal.

Speaking just in general, since one should not deal with

specific cases, one may say that moral rules pose tricky problems. Adopted for worthy motives, they may nevertheless be responsible for evil that good men do. New circumstances call for new actions that the rule doesn't allow for, and too strict an interpretation of the rule may prevent a higher righteousness.

Sometimes, men being what they are, the motive for following the rule may even change a bit, and what begins as a restraint against doing what we think we shouldn't do may end as an excuse for not doing what we ought to do.

4. PIETY ALONG THE POTOMAC

August 17, 1954

The manifestations of religion in Washington have become pretty thick. We have had opening prayers, Bible breakfasts, special church services, prayer groups, a "Back to God" crusade, and campaign speeches on "spiritual values"; now we have added a postage stamp, a proposed Constitutional amendment, and a change in the Pledge of Allegiance. The Pledge, which has served well enough in times more pious than ours, has now had its rhythm upset but its anti-Communist spirituality improved by the insertion of the phrase "under God." The Postmaster General has held a dedication ceremony, at which the President and the Secretary of State explained about spiritual values and such, to launch a new red, white, and blue eight-cent postage stamp bearing the motto "In God We Trust." A bill has been introduced directing the post office to cancel mail with the slogan "Pray for Peace." (The devout, in place of daily devotions, can just read what is stuck and stamped all over the letters in their mail.)

The inaugural prayer of the President now hangs under glass on the wall of the Vice-President's office, just as "God Bless Our Home" or the Golden Rule used to hang in other places. After his election, the President joined a church. To one of the many church groups he has met with he said that he prefers his preachers to be vigorous and forthright in defense of their position. (None of the visiting clergymen thought to say that he prefers his Presidents that way too.) Cabinet meetings are now said to be started with prayer. (An irreverent Washington joke ends, "Dammit, we forgot the opening prayer.") *Life* Magazine's article on the President's religion reports an increased attendance at Senate, House, and departmental prayer groups. (It also reports the complaint that these groups seem "to enjoy listening to lay speakers who easily equate piety with personal prosperity.") For the Very Big Men there are the annual prayer breakfasts of the International Council of Christian Laymen with grapefruit, scrambled eggs, a New Testament reading by Vice-President Nixon, and the singing of one of the President's favorite hymns, "What a Friend We Have in Jesus."

Elmer Davis wrote about Independence Day a year ago: "The greatest demonstration of the religious character of this administration came on July Fourth, which the President told us all to spend as a day of penance and prayer. Then he himself caught four fish in the morning, played eighteen holes of golf in the afternoon, and spent the evening at the bridge table."

To note all this in a deflationary tone is not to say that religion and politics don't mix. Politicians should develop deeper religious convictions, and religious folk should develop wiser political convictions; both need to relate political duties to religious faith — but not in an unqualified and public way that confuses the absolute and emotional loyalties of religion with the relative and shifting loyalties of politics.

Most of the problems with the public sort of thing are illustrated in the following story from the New York *Times* of January 19, 1953:

> Carpenters raced against time in a remote corner of the National Guard Armory here today to complete an added starter to the procession of floats in Tuesday's Inaugural Parade. To the three men who conceived the idea it is known as "God's Float." They hope it will come to be known as such throughout the world.
>
> Last week the floats were nearing completion in the armory basement. Then it was discovered by a parade official that nowhere was there to be any representation that this was a nation whose people believed in God.
>
> Then, in keeping with the Biblical precept, inaugural officials decided that this — the last float conceived — should be the first in the order of march.
>
> It will have constructed on its base a central edifice denoting a place of worship. The side aprons will carry greatly enlarged photographs of churches and other scenes of worship. In Gothic script on the sides and ends of the float will appear the legends, "Freedom of Worship" and "In God We Trust."

The object of devotion for this float is "religion." The faith is not in God but in faith; we worship our own worshiping. The symbols are "greatly enlarged photographs" of "scenes of worship."

Of the monstrosity which resulted from this particular effort the *Episcopal Churchnews* wrote: "Remember the float representing religion in President Eisenhower's inaugural parade? Standing for all religions, it had the symbols of none, and it looked like nothing whatsoever in Heaven above, or in the

earth beneath, except possibly an oversized model of a de-
formed molar left over from some dental exhibit."

Since this is official religion in a land without an official religion it cannot be very deep. The careful inoffensiveness of
public office leads straight to the semi-secular religion or the
semi-religious secularism which is both a convenient compromise among the wide variety of positions to which officialdom
must be attentive and a very popular position in its own right.

The content of official religion is bound to be thin; the commitment to it is also apt to be hollow now and then. Where
everybody professionally believes something, then for some the
belief may be a bit more professional than real. A float may
not represent a faith integral to the participants' lives, but
rather the prudent recollection by a functionary of what the
public would expect. Religion is now very popular, and the
politician's business is to know and to follow what is popular.
Letters, according to the *Times* amounting to thousands daily,
"flooded Congress" in support of the change in the Pledge.
Newspapers (prominent among them the Hearst chain) and
radio commentators endorsed it, and organizations like the
Knights of Columbus gave it hearty support.

Too often this dubious mixture of patriotism and religion
serves the purposes of a conservative social philosophy, as
when the old ways in faith bless the old ways in economics.
There may be a touch of this blessed conservatism, and there
certainly is more than a touch of blessed nationalism, in the
American Legion's "Back to God" crusade.

Mr. Nixon, speaking on behalf of it, is apparently convinced,
like the Legion, that the direction in which God is to be found
is "back." Mr. Nixon's remarks at that time illustrate a constant theme of Washington piety: Promote religion because it
is useful to the nation in fighting Communism. He emphasized that the country's greatest asset in fighting Communism

is its spiritual heritage. The note of pride and invidious self-congratulation for this "advantage" became very plain in his list of things we have that they do not. "Among the great privileges that we enjoy is the privilege of hearing President Eisenhower pray at the beginning of his inauguration. That could not happen in half the world today. We also have the privilege of attending the churches of our choice. That, too, could not happen in half the world today." Mr. Nixon called free worship "our greatest defense against enemies from without"; Mr. Eisenhower on a radio-TV program launching the crusade called faith "our surest strength, our greatest resource." In his remarks on the Pledge he said, "We shall constantly strengthen those spiritual weapons which forever will be our country's most powerful resource, in peace or in war." This reduction of religion to a national "resource," "advantage," "strength," and "weapon," especially useful for anti-Communist purposes, received perhaps its perfect expression from the perfect folk hero for the devotees of such an outlook, J. Edgar Hoover, when he wrote, "Since Communists are anti-God, encourage your child to be active in the church."

Officialdom prefers religion which is useful for national purposes, but undemanding and uncomplicated in itself. It also wants religion which is negotiable to the widest possible public. Therefore the official faith is easily impressed with the spread of any simple external sign of religion, however empty of content. The President praised the Legion's "Back to God" movement as a "positive act," and he said of the postage stamp that "the sender can feel he has done something positive and constructive." His picture of the result of the addition of two words to the Pledge also seems a little extravagant: "From this day forward, the millions of our school children will daily proclaim in every city and town, every village and rural school house, the dedication of our nation and our people to the Almighty. To anyone who truly loves America, nothing could be more inspiring than to contemplate this rededication of our youth, on each school morning, to our country's true meaning."

But two more words in chorus each morning represent no such dedication, nor does Congress's passing the bill to change the Pledge constitute a dedication; sending a stamp is nothing "constructive," and a big promotion campaign with placards saying "Go to Church" is not an especially "positive act."

All religious affirmations are in danger of standing in contradiction to the life that is lived under them, but none more so than these general, inoffensive, and externalized ones which are put together for public purposes.

What is affirmed often stands in ironic contrast to what is otherwise being done and thought and said.

An old cartoon by Robert Day in the *New Yorker* illustrates what I mean: A street-corner evangelist whose sign reads LOVE THY NEIGHBOR shouts to a competitor, "I'm telling you for the last time — keep the hell off this corner!"

5. SENATOR NEELY'S MISTAKE

1955

On March 28, 1955, Senator Matthew M. Neely, an elderly West Virginia Democrat, included in a speech to the United Auto Workers in Cleveland a passing critical reference to the President's churchgoing, and to his never having joined a church until he was President. The national response to this one brief reference was staggering: immense, immediate, and altogether negative. With his one sharp phrase about the President's religion Senator Neely evoked an outraged response by Republicans, the strained silence of many of his own Democratic colleagues, and an angry editorial and cartoon attack upon himself. He received a monumental outpouring of mail, overwhelmingly unfavorable, which called him, among other, less printable things, an "ugly old magpie"; "you stinking swine"; "white trash from the hills"; "pig-faced"; and a "bartender in a cheap bar." "I am a coal miner," said one letter; "have always voted for you but no more. You killed yourself politically." "Out of bounds." "Bad taste." "New political low." "Beyond the pale." "Vicious smear." Some letters contented themselves with defense ("As I live in the Eisenhower home territory I know how Christian the Eisenhowers have always been"); others were rather more pointedly invidious, like the one enclosing a picture of the Eisenhowers praying and asking "See anything wrong with this, Senator? He's not praying to John L. Lewis, you know, as you no doubt would be in a similar pose."

Senator Neely himself, wounded by the intensity and antagonism of the response, protested: "I would do the same thing if it were Harry Truman." For a while he collected items seeming to indicate the use of the President's religion for partisan purposes and entertained the thought of a Senate speech which would respond to the critics of his remarks. President Eisenhower's heart attack in September 1955, however, ended that idea. "When God puts His hand on a man," said the Senator, "Matthew Neely takes his away." One detected a hint of relief that the greater hand had intervened, for Matthew Neely's had picked up a very hot potato indeed.

6. GOLDEN MOMENT

1956

After the delegates had gathered for the first night of the Republican convention in San Francisco, and after the keynote

speech had ended with words about faith and spirit, the chairman introduced motion picture actress Irene Dunne. She
came forward with a very earnest manner, and began, in fact
rather tremulously, to recite the prayer that President Eisenhower had given at his inauguration in 1952. While she re-
cited it to the millions watching on television, violins beneath
her voice played "America the Beautiful," and the television
cameras panned to the sunset on the Pacific, out at the Golden
Gate. (Apparently this part of the program had been timed to
correspond to that event.)

The Republican National Committee, an agency by nature
peculiarly susceptible to the attractions of the author of the
prayer, was once moved to say that President Eisenhower "is
not only the political leader, but the spiritual leader of our
times." Some critical observers — notably Adlai Stevenson —
following up on that thought in a different tone of voice, said
of the San Francisco gathering that it seemed to be more a
coronation than a political convention. Having been fascinated
by the British coronation and startled to see that it was both
a national and a religious ceremony, perhaps we wanted to
have — in our own rather different way, of course — our
coronation, too.

But then one must remember that the planning committee
for the convention had a problem. With no contest for the
Presidential nomination, what *should* they do with all that free
television time?

7. THE BIPARTISANSHIP OF VICUNAS

June 27, 1958

One should not add to the discomfiture of the Republicans
over that almost perfect case of poetic justice, the Sherman

Adams episode, or to the unholy glee of the Democrats on discovering a Goldfine. One may observe, however, that they seem to be missing the main point. The lesson to be learned from the incident is not, necessarily, that one should always pay one's own hotel bills, or that one should flee like a wild, hunted thing from millionaires bearing gifts; or that a President should not come to "need" any assistant so much that he can't get along without him — though no doubt there are some useful things to be learned along those lines. The real lesson, rather, is that "corruption" always has been vastly overworked as a partisan and a political weapon. When Democrat Mike DiSalle ran for an Ohio Senate seat in the mink coat year of 1952 somebody asked him whether "corruption" would be an issue in the campaign. "I suppose so," he said, "but I don't know who's going to take the affirmative."

It is now clear, in the vicuna coat year of 1958, that it is a mistake for anyone to take a self-righteously partisan negative on that conveniently one-sided matter. But now both parties are at it again, their roles reversed, exploiting that American love of a cozy little personal "moral" issue. Rather than think about the national budget, we prefer to hear about somebody's family budget or hotel bill, which, even though the amounts seem a little high, are still within range of ordinary experience. We like the relatively simple and personal issues on which neat lines of "right" and "wrong" seem easy to draw; on high finance and intercontinental missiles it is hard to know where to stand, but on "influence-peddling" and oriental rugs it is easy.

The Republicans, who played this game for all its worth, are now being paid in kind, but unfortunately they don't seem to have learned anything. In his two big chances the chief moral crusader has used the wrong test. On the Nixon Fund he appealed to public opinion, and in the Adams case he has appealed to personal need, neither of which is a particularly elegant standard. In their defense of Adams the Republicans have not allowed themselves to admit that there are some shared, bipartisan human problems here — problems that are not simple, that root partly in our big, complicated institutions, partly in the absence of standards, partly in the nature of the human animal. Instead they have gone back to their claims that they are somehow a different breed, that *their* man *must* have, as the New York *Herald Tribune* put it, "total integrity."

The *Herald Tribune* even tried to use the axiomatic goodness of the President as a transferable commodity: "The heart of the matter," they said, "is that Dwight Eisenhower has the faith, trust, and affection of the American people . . . If the American people place such faith and trust in the President, he is entitled to ask them to place equal faith and trust in those whom he chooses . . . No more needs to be said." A lot more needs to be said. We do not know about the ethical practices of these fellows but their ethical arguments are dubious.

We are as tired of the politics of the house furnishings, appliances, phone calls, and haberdashery of various public figures as, presumably, the Republican leaders now have come to be. But when they say that too much is made of the Adams case, that the headlines are too big, that we ought to "get back to work," that there are other, "life and death problems to confront," our memories of 1952 come flooding back. We agree with what they now say, but we would not defend to the death *their* right to say it.

8. FROM SUASION TO DISSUASION
September 15, 1958

It has long been apparent that Mr. Eisenhower's understanding of society, like everything else about him, is very American. But now it appears that the President represents the classic American social ethic not at its best but at something nearer the other pole. Nothing reveals this more than the school segregation issue.

It first appeared that the President represented the rather naïve, but nevertheless tolerable, outlook of a traditional moralism. He seemed, like much of America and of the American church traditionally, to skip over matters of social structure and to expect instead that great sweeping changes would come about through a "change of heart." He seemed to have that trust in moral exhortation and in the sudden change in the will of men that has particularly marked American pietism. About the school segregation question he would say constantly that matters like this could not be settled by "mere law," and that there must be a change within.

This view underestimates the resistant force that a deep social habit (like racial discrimination) can present; it lacks a sense of social continuity, and therefore, instead of planning, responds to each crisis (like Little Rock) as it arises; it locates evil in the will of a few individuals (like Faubus) who can be called to Newport and supposedly charmed into goodness; it tends to become just an excuse for *not* doing what law or force can and must do. When disappointed it can then belatedly and suddenly turn to the angry use of physical force, justified by the highest moral claims (as in traditional American responses to war). The President's angry switch from platitudes to paratroops last fall was an example of the way an overtrust in persuasion turns suddenly to blunt force. If one's view of power is not sufficiently calibrated, then one overdoes things one way or another.

Nevertheless this heritage is better than a cynical alternative which would give no place to the moral will. At its best, and in the right places, this traditional morality can be effective. Where there are changeable attitudes and dramatic ills, the straight-out appeal to the conscience can play a significant role. From abolitionist days to the present, race relations has been such an issue.

But with the Presidential press conferences of late August one began to wonder whether in the high places there was even the limited merit of this pietist tradition. Though there was mention of moral suasion, there wasn't any. Though there was mention of the changes of heart that must come, nothing was said to bring them about. Though reference was made to education and reason, there was no educating or reasoning. The matter was left to public opinion, as though that opinion was formed in a vacuum.

In the August 20 press conference Mr. Eisenhower explicitly ruled himself out of the struggles of the heart. He said it would not do for him to state his position on the moral issue of the case, because this might interfere with his role in enforcing the law. He represented himself as the executive of the laws in the abstract and, by that role, forbidden to exercise moral leadership. He let a situation develop, as he did in the McCarthy case, in which the opposing forces have the initiative and the public attention, to reassure or intimidate the wavering and mobilize supporters, while he forswears participation in the very struggle of persuasion and opinion to which he himself has left the issue.

Then, in the August 27 press conference, he took another step. He not only aided anti-integration by silence; he now aided it by explicit statement. He said "slower." With the issue drawn, the word could only serve to discourage integrationists and encourage the supporters of the segregation system. The great advocate of moral suasion on this issue himself exercised moral dissuasion.

9. POLITICS IS SO CONFUSING

November 27, 1958

For six years now, Mr. Eisenhower has been working at this political thing, and he doesn't seem to be getting much closer to understanding it than when he started. In the baffled remarks at his press conference on the morning after the elections, he showed once more what a wonderful confusion he can make of it all — a quite representative confusion, and therefore related to his own great personal appeal but not of much use in a political way to anyone else.

His remarks came at the start of that struggle which always follows each election, the struggle to interpret the results. Sometimes this battle can be almost as intense and as important as the one that preceded it: policies, candidates, and factions can win and lose by having victory or defeat convincingly ascribed to them. Among the victors, each group tries to find its own principles responsible for the victory; in this case, Johnsonian moderation, for example, or forthright liberalism. ("The Democratic Party has won a mandate," said Mr. Stevenson, possibly to the surprise of some dairy farmers and others, "to provide the thoughtful and creative leadership our nation needs in this dangerous time.")

The struggle among the vanquished is even more intense, each faction trying to find the other one responsible for the defeat. While in one column of the New York *Herald Tribune* Roscoe Drummond finds modern Republicanism strong even in the party's loss, just a column away David Lawrence insists that Republicans can't win when their modernism keeps hordes of true conservatives home from the polls. (The election provided a clue to the whereabouts of those hidden hordes of Taftian Republicans, by the way; they seem to be secreted somewhere in the mesas of Arizona.)

At 7:45 on the evening after the election, Edward R. Murrow explained that the clearest meaning in the election was the defeat of conservative Republicanism, but three-quarters of an hour earlier Fulton Lewis, Jr., had advanced a much more striking, if less convincing, argument exactly to the contrary. The Republicans won, he said, when they were independent of Eisenhower and true to Republican principles (Goldwater, Hruska, and — well — Keating), and they lost when they tried to follow Eisenhower into a hyphenated me-too "modern" Republicanism indistinguishable from Democratic radicalism (Thye, Potter, Payne, and even Watkins). Mr. Lewis managed somehow to wind this interpretation around the defeat of Malone, Barrett, and Bricker (in these races there was a close finish, or overconfidence, or something) and the victory of Rockefeller and Scott (these didn't involve national issues). Never mind about Knowland. Mr. Lewis's whole analysis was a work of awe-inspiring ingenuity.

Mr. Eisenhower's interpretation was impressive for quite different reasons. Like Mr. Lewis, he is consistent, but his consistency serves no Republican faction. Though verbally firm in his desire to promote a "modern Republicanism," he was his usual amorphous self in relating that desire to the election returns. His remarks really link him not to a new Republicanism but to an old Americanism: to the sturdy tradition that finds politics baffling and tries to deal with its shifting and limited conflicts over policy with huge, static, noncontroversial, and usually inapplicable words about character, personal relations, and broad (very broad) principle.

One could see it in the President's repeated insistence that he had been "preaching" exactly the same thing for six years, as though the constancy of his own rhetoric ought to have been matched by an equally constant support on the part of the public, and as though the purity of doctrine preached, rather than the effect of action taken or not taken, should have been the test. One could see it, too, in the perplexed reference to a "complete reversal" in 1958 of the 1956 results: there is a curious pathos in this popular hero's lack of comprehension of the non-political bases of his own victories. Apparently he will continue to the end to believe that his good American friends voted not for him (to believe that, he said after the 1956 election, would be "egotistical") but for the "principles" of "modern Republicanism." How difficult that would be was clear from the same press conference: Republicanism seemed to consist in being for peace, in keeping the economy on an even keel, and — with rather sudden urgency — in non-spending; modernity seemed to extend all the way over to John Bricker.

That last matter really showed in a clear light Mr. Eisenhower's trouble with the mysteries of politics. Asked whether the absence of such men as Senators Malone and Bricker might not actually make it easier to pass some programs of his own, such as foreign aid, he said he would not want to predict about that. Except for the one thing of the Bricker amendment, he felt that he and the Senator were rather in the same camp; certainly their personal relations were friendly, and he wasn't going to do anything so tasteless and unfriendly as actually to look up the man's voting record.

10. THE END OF THE MIDDLE
OF THE ROAD

February 16, 1959

The last acts of the drama, like the budget he presents this
year, find Mr. Eisenhower well out of the middle of the road.
That never was a very satisfactory traveling place — it is
crowded, wide and ambiguous as to destination. Almost everyone is out there in the middle of some road: all the candidates
in both parties now jockeying for position in the Presidential
Derby are to be found within some enlarged middle.

Mr. Eisenhower still speaks occasionally in the tones of his
earlier middling. When he is criticized, for example, he seems
to think that there is some sign of virtue in being hit from both
sides. His response to the rumblings against him by the Taft
Republicans in Des Moines was to say rather complacently
that the man who stands in the middle must expect to take it
from both sides.

But despite these echoes of an earlier policy of being liberal
on Mondays, Wednesdays and Fridays and conservative on
Tuesdays, Thursdays and Saturdays — or whatever it was —
the budget, and the campaign that preceded it, have little of
the great middling effort built around the President's suprapolitical personality. The budget is an issue on which the
Administration has taken a stand. Among the evils that face
us, it has chosen plainly to say that the most dangerous is in-
flation. Among the objectives to which federal economic
policy might be directed, it has chosen that of the balanced
budget.

It is at least good to have the Administration far enough out
of the middle of the road to disagree with it unequivocally.

Part II

Can Government Be Merchandised?

October 27, 1953

A PROMINENT member of the "Dewey team" complained after the Governor's first eighteen-hour television show, in 1950, that it was disgraceful that the distinguished governor of a great state (I think that's the way it goes) should have to appear in such a public relations stunt. An advertising man who helped to arrange the "telethon" quoted Jimmy Durante in reply: "Dem's da conditions dat prevail."

Da conditions have come to prevail, since then, more and more, for public relations men and their close relatives, advertising men, have been moving into politics in a big way. Their activities, which hitherto have included tasks like creating memorable headgear for candidate Kefauver, devising such edifying slogans as "You never had it so good" and "The voluntary way is the American Way," and figuring out new places to print the phrase "I Like Ike," have now come to include the planning of entire campaigns and even, most recently, the conduct of government.

Governor Dewey may owe an extraordinary debt to such professional public relations, for it is said that after his defeat in 1948 an exhaustive investigation of his public personality by an advertising agency led to the redesigning of his mustache. Whether it was this singular service or the hundred thousand votes he admitted the telethon had gained for him, something plainly ended whatever scruples he may have had about public relations in politics. In 1952 he used all kinds of props and twists and hammed it up on each new television production number his advertising agency worked out for him. His question-and-answer programs with prearranged questions from selected ordinary people, his comedy programs about "Harry's Haunted House," and his commentary programs on which he was Deeply Shocked each week at what the Democrats had done showed how thoroughly the distinguished governor of a great state was willing to accept the ad-men's judgment as to the conditions that prevail.

A public relations man may defend his new role in politics by saying that he just takes good political ideas that haven't gone across and makes them go across. The editor of *Tide,* an advertising and sales trade publication, remarked during the past campaign, ". . . advertising . . . demonstrated beyond question that it can sell a good idea as successfully as it can sell a good product." But this statement omits the rather important fact that it can do the same for a *bad* idea. And advertising is not simply neutral as to whether the idea is good or bad, but has a bias within it.

I don't mean whatever biases there may be in advertising men and agencies as a result of their relation to the business community and its politics. I mean the bias in the nature of advertising itself. It is this bias of which some public relations men in politics seem spectacularly unaware. They seem not to see that the media over which you say something and the devices by which you say it alter what you say.

The advertising man tells the politician to make the argument quick and simple, without any unpleasant complexities. (VOICE: Mr. Eisenhower, what about the high cost of living?

EISENHOWER: My wife, Mamie, worries about the same thing. I tell her it's our job to change that on November 4th.) He says the appeal must be basic and unmistakable. ("The farmer's farming every day, making money and that ain't hay. CLAP! CLAP! Don't let 'em take it away!")

Qualifications must be carefully subordinated to clear, positive, unequivocal promises. (VOICE: Mr. Eisenhower, can you bring taxes down? EISENHOWER: Yes. We will work to cut billions in Washington spending, and bring your taxes down.) The opposition between the two parties must be made dramatic and absolute. ("They'll promise you the sky. They'll promise you the earth! But what's a Republican's promise worth?") Fearful and tragic events are to be associated with the Opposition. (VOICE: General, the Democrats are telling me I never had it so good. EISENHOWER: Can that be true when America is billions in debt, when prices have doubled, when taxes break our backs, and we are still fighting in Korea? It is tragic. It is time for a change.) Familiar symbols of home and prestige must be associated with the client. ("The Democratic party took apples off the streets and put apple pie on the table. Whenever history puts them to the test, Americans will always choose the best.") The advertiser tells the politician that examples should be memorable, whether or not they are illuminating or representative. (VOICE: General, just how bad is waste in Washington? EISENHOWER: How bad? Recently, just one government bureau actually lost four hundred million dollars and not even the FBI can find it. It's *really* time for a change.)

Clem Whitaker, partner in the California advertising firm of Whitaker and Baxter, which conducted the American Medical Association's successful multi-million-dollar campaign to eliminate national health insurance ("socialized medicine") from the alternatives politically available to the American people, is one of the most outspoken of the new public relations men in politics. Whitaker has drawn up an apparently definitive list of the grand strategies of political campaigns built on public relations techniques: ". . . you can interest voters if you put on a fight. No matter what the fight, *fight for something* . . . You may wonder if that is the only technique in campaigning. It isn't the only one. There are two. The average American also likes to be entertained . . . He likes the movies and he likes fireworks and parades. So if you can't fight, put on a show!"

A public relations man in politics may say he is only doing better what politicians have always done. But though the "old-style" politician often did oversimplify and use slogans and appeal to fear and greed, he does not seem to have done this quite so systematically or so effectively as the modern advertisers in politics. He did not have the dominating control of the sources of opinion that the modern national "mass media" advertiser can enjoy, nor the habits of mind that come from "selling" a mass market. And he had a restraining set of pressures on him to which some of the political advertising men do not seem to be subject; at least he had to pay some attention to facts. His campaigns may have lacked moxie, but he had to deal with interests of his constituents, which were real and which were independent of his manipulation. He could not, as a memorandum from one public relations firm advised its agents to do, "create situations of reality"; he had to fit his actions to a reality that already existed. He could not engage in what public relations man Edward L. Bernays has described as the "engineering of public consent"; he had to let the public engineer its own consent.

Mr. Whitaker has said that managing campaigns, now becoming "a mature, well-managed business, *founded on sound public relations principles,* and using every technique of modern-day advertising," is "no longer a hit-or-miss business, directed by broken-down politicians." But it is not clear that these new PR men like Mr. Whitaker are an improvement over even the "broken-down" politicians. No politicians, for instance, could have the adman's freewheeling auxiliary relationship to politics, thinking up slogans at "brainstorm meetings" for clients with the money to pay for them. The politicians were potential public officials and as such had to shape their relationship to the public to some extent in accord with their ability to act as a part of a government. Many of them, in their quaint, broken-down way, have had a genuine interest in public policy. Occasionally one could even discern, in some of them, an honest conviction. They rarely approached the immaculate amorality of the political public relations man who, admitting that his candidate did not know anything about anything, said: "Let's consider this campaign clinically. After all, you don't criticize a brain surgeon's technique just because he operates on a criminal."

The public relations man tends to work backwards, from desired effect to technique to content. If present tendencies continue, we may get political campaigns tailored to fit the requirements of public relations and then government tailored to fit the requirements of the campaign.

Clem Whitaker has a consoling thought to offer on this score: ". . . whatever technique we use, in the end we always come back to Lincoln's fundamental — public sentiment is everything. If sometimes we go to extremes to create that sentiment, we can recall that some of the greatest statesmen in American history went to extremes, too." Going to extremes has testimonials from top-brand-name statesmen, and never mind whether Mr. Whitaker's extremes are quite the same as Mr. Lincoln's.

It is a bit hard to tell at this distance just what Lincoln meant by his statement "public sentiment is everything," but it is clear what Whitaker, who quotes it fondly, means. He means that public sentiment is *everything*. Other facts of the political world, such as the structure of Congress, the size of armies, the location of oil, national beliefs that run deeper than the mood of the moment — these are not very important, and can easily be controlled by the proper manipulation of public sentiment.

Even a new character for a candidate can be created synthetically, by a nickname, a slogan, the right profile, or a redesigned mustache. Unfortunately for the public relations man, however, the realities behind the illusions he builds sometimes do break through to spoil things. The candidate's character cannot always be entirely concealed by his public relations man. This exasperates Mr. Whitaker: ". . . an automobile . . . can't object to your sales talk, and if you step on the starter, it usually runs. A candidate, on the other hand, can and does talk back — and can sometimes talk you out of an election, despite the best you can do in campaign headquarters."

Mr. Whitaker explains that public relations campaigners like himself have a problem with a candidate's "willingness or unwillingness to hew to the line on the plan of strategy which has been worked out . . . his ability or inability to measure up to the character you give him by your carefully prepared build-up." Apparently some old-fashioned candidates still want to hew to their own line rather than the adman's, and present to the public their own character rather than that given by Mr. Whitaker's "carefully prepared build-up."

In this revealing statement by Miss Baxter, Mr. Whitaker's

partner in "Campaigns, Inc." to her fellow practitioners of this new art, notice her view of the public, and of democracy, and of the public relations man:

> It's because the public relations profession, and its allied professions, know something about presenting abstract ideas, in attractive form, to masses of people who are too occupied with their daily lives to think analytically on their own account, that the average man today is in a position to know more about the trends of human affairs than ever in history . . . You are helping him to understand your clients and their problems, their ideals. You are helping him to be a better citizen.

The techniques by which some public relations people help us to be better citizens — those of us too occupied with our daily lives to think analytically on our own account — now include, for an example, the saturation radio-TV spot campaign, brought to the service of the nation in last year's Republican campaign. The plan for this operation, How to insure an Eisenhower victory in November, listed these advantages of concentrating the spot announcements in the last three weeks: "1. It gives maximum effectiveness of penetration and recall without becoming deadly to the listener and viewer. 2. It delivers the maximum just before the election. 3. It occurs at too late a date for effective Democratic rebuttal." (Since this memorandum makes the regrettable slip of calling the Democratic Party by its name, it must have been another agency which struck a blow for decency in government by deciding that Republican orators should henceforth call the Democratic Party the "Democrat" Party.) The spot-campaign people were concerned with higher things, a "special, all out effort to switch forty-nine counties in twelve states and with it the election to Eisenhower." When I asked the head of the advertising agency that handled the Democratic Party's account about this satura-

tion spot campaign, he seemed worried only that I might think
the Republicans had stolen a march on him. "We had the idea
for a saturation spot campaign long before the Republicans,"
he protested, "but we couldn't get the money."

Another way the public is brought to understand the client's
ideals is by hearing them whether it wants to or not. For example, the Republican advertisers are well satisfied that they
made a net gain last year over the Democrats by purchasing
the higher priced time already allocated to top TV performers.
A man who arranges such political programs explained it to
me: "A viewer tunes in to see Arthur Godfrey, but in place of
Godfrey there is our program, and since there *are no top
programs opposite Godfrey* he has to come back to us!" Thus
is the public "delivered" to be taught about trends in human
affairs.

To one outside public relations and its allied professions,
capturing, delivering, and saturating the public would appear
to be rather the opposite of helping it to know human affairs
and understand ideals. In a way it would seem that the better
the public relations, the wider the gap between the public's
emotional approval of the client and the public's rational
understanding of the reasons *why* it approves of the client.
The advertising man's habit and purpose is to go beneath the
reason to build strong emotional attachments to what he is
selling, by associating it with all good symbols, relevant or not.
Thus, it seems from the pictures in the advertisements that
toothpaste has not only brightened the young lady's teeth but
also papered the walls, straightened the room, and introduced
her to a smashingly handsome young man. The advertiser's
victim automatically calls the toothpaste's name when she
goes to the drugstore.

Such techniques, transferred to politics, help the candidate to do "scientifically" what he has always tried to do, in his old fumbling, uncertain ways. He can say something without saying it. His advertising can systematically create an impression that goes well beyond any direct claim he would make and have to stand by. The most striking example of such public relations is the treatment of the Korean war by the Republicans last year, and in particular Mr. Eisenhower's "I will go to Korea" speech. In millions of American homes, voters had a deep and emotional *impression* that Eisenhower would end the Korean war, but the Eisenhower forces could rightly say that they never directly made any such claim. It was a triumph of the manipulation of public sentiment.

The Eisenhower movement, born and nurtured in the smooth new world of public relations, is the biggest client yet persuaded of the prevailing conditions. Not only from Governor Dewey and his team but also from the alert businessmen who flocked to the banner, the crusade came to understand how tough a "selling" job the Republicans had, and how useful modern "scientific" selling practices could be for such a tough job. During the primary campaign Senator Taft complained that some top executives, even against their own inclination, were supporting Eisenhower on the advice of their corporations' public relations men. Of the convention at which Mr. Eisenhower was nominated, *Tide* wrote in its snappy newsletter: "The *Republican convention* next week will almost be *a convention of advertising and public relations men*. An amazing number are attending . . ." A group of public relations men, called the "Eisenhower-Nixon Research Service," takes credit for the first big Eisenhower victory, for it gave the "Fair Play" amendment its felicitous name and planned the triumphantly successful buildup of public support of the Eisenhower side in that crucial convention fight.

During the campaign the same group chose, named, and pushed the "captive candidate" theme against Stevenson, but this was only one of many public relations groups working for Eisenhower. Three advertising agencies had a hand in the campaign: the Kudner agency, which was originally given the Republican account; Batten, Barton, Durstine & Osborn, which joined the crusade early in September and came to handle all radio and TV for the General; and the Bates agency, one of whose executives thought up the much debated saturation spot campaign.

But the Eisenhower movement did not stop its use of public relations techniques on Election Day; the "conditions" apparently "prevail" not only for campaigns but also for governments. An article on "The GOP's 'PR'" in the *Wall Street Journal* late in February said: ". . . the Eisenhower forces already have a fair claim to the title of the most-public-relations-conscious-administration in history. . . . This heavier-than-ever accent on 'scientific' public relations techniques crops up all over the place. . . ."

The *Journal* story concentrated on the Eisenhower-Nixon Research Service, now renamed the Research Associates, and their proposal of a "carefully-calculated, Government-wide effort to cultivate the public" with methods which the *Journal* reporter said were "reminiscent of those employed by a private company . . ." The plan was presented in a "fascinating brochure . . . handsomely gotten up in a black loose-leaf notebook with cellophane-covered pages, a gaudy layout, and the word 'Confidential' stamped on the front," which was reported to have found its way to the bedside table of the President and also to Vice-President Nixon and Postmaster General Summerfield.

A more recent story in the *Wall Street Journal* reported that

"Eisenhower & Co. have opened a new sales department right in the White House. The new division of the Republican Administration is headed by a man President Eisenhower privately calls 'the greatest salesman in the world' — the Seattle mortgage banker, Walter Williams . . ." Mr. Williams, who is also Under Secretary of Commerce, will try in this new job "to 'sell' the President's policies to the public — and tout his achievements." As the *Journal* story observed, ". . . the Eisenhower forces, a lot of them former businessmen, simply believe in a little salesmanship."

This salesmanship was nowhere more evident than in the President's TV report in June to the people of the nation he governs. It was planned, rehearsed, and presented under the professional supervision of B.B.D. & O.

Tide reports that Bernard C. Duffy, head of B.B.D. & O., said of the campaign last fall that Republican strategy centered on merchandising Eisenhower's frankness, honesty, and integrity, his sincere and wholesome approach. The strategy by which the candidate was "merchandised" was used again in June to "merchandise" the President. B.B.D. & O.'s best techniques of television advertising were employed to bring the President and his Cabinet to the people, to tell them about how the roof was not leaking. It was as though, having created during the campaign the TV character Likeable Ike, his sponsors found it expedient to continue the installments of his adventures. *Advertising Agency* Magazine quoted Mr. Duffy's satisfied comment: "One of our best shows."

This adman's "show" did not insist that the public make controversial decisions about world policy. Instead the implied view of the public was that of a docile, harmonious family, waiting to be told a few fascinating facts about its government by Likeable Ike and his swell friends. Government appeared as

a merely technical and administrative matter: "What you're
concerned about is that the house is in good order" — about
which there is, of course, harmonious agreement. "Now, everybody helps to do that, everybody in the family." Yes, everything is being well handled by these dandy people we have in
government: "Since government is just people, you have seen
the kind of people that are trying to solve these things for you."

There was no suggestion that there might be at stake serious
questions of value about which the public had to decide.
Rather, Herb and George, and Mr. Benson, who was a farmer
himself, and Mrs. Hobby, whose job was a woman's in the
home, just read lines to show the fascinating but easily understandable Romance of Government. Through their edifying
discourses ran homey little advertising gimmicks — the basket
of mail from which "we get our ideas"; a letter from a lady in
Pawtucket; 8 to 1 approval of the entire program; a chart showing Mr. Benson's travels; a mention of Derby, Kansas, and
Limestone, Maine. The "points of interest" chattily described
were all assumed to be completely under control by the genial
and efficient new managers of the business — "I'm going over
to Bermuda to meet with some of our friends and talk over
these things"; "Well, now, of course, George, we know we're
going to stop this" — and the public can rest easy, assured that
"We've done something and are now doing things to repair the
holes in the roof and keep the fences mended."

Bill Tyler, who writes a column in *Advertising Agency* Magazine called "Copy Clinic," had the following illuminating
comment:

> Undoubtedly the most effective commercial of the month
> was the President's TV appearance around the first of June . . .
> It closely followed the pattern of an agency new-business solici-
> tation. The President let each department head, armed with

slides, present the story of his branch of the business. Then he wrapped the whole thing up in a masterful manner and asked for the order. As a TV salesman, we think you will agree, Dwight Eisenhower has few peers . . .

Members of the Eisenhower Administration themselves sometimes seem to conceive the relationship of the government to the people in advertising terms. The *Wall Street Journal* quoted this statement from a high official, which the President is said to endorse, explaining the new White House sales office: "We all suddenly realized we were busy manufacturing a product down here, but nobody was selling it." One of the President's top aides sent a memorandum to all government personnel who deal with foreign policy just before the President's important April 16 speech to the American Newspaper Publishers Association. The memorandum described an elaborate plan to publicize the speech around the world, and it called this promotion of a major address of the President of the United States "merchandising-in-depth."

The differences between selling a product in a market and choosing public policies in a democracy may not be immediately apparent to some advertising people. The consumer acts as an individual and may be able to defend himself against high pressure and the gullibility of his neighbor — by consumer resistance or buying different products (at least, that is the theory). But the citizen *must* live under the government that he helps to select, and it can make ultimate claims upon him. The political issue is the health and direction of the whole community, not just the satisfaction of an individual consumer's desire. And the seat of decision in democratic politics should be the deliberating reason and conscience of a public, not the manipulated passion and interest of a crowd. Of course our democratic politics rarely works the way that it is supposed to; but that is all the more reason for not wanting it to be controlled by those who do not even know what that is.

The public relations man says these other conditions prevail, and we might as well accept them. But it is possible that conditions he likes are not quite as prevalent as he says. In the 1952 campaign the Republicans were selling the public something which it very much wanted to "buy," a change and a hero. By evoking distaste in some quarters, the "Ike" advertising may even have helped the Opposition. In the face of the overwhelming odds, the significant evidence about public relations from the 1952 campaign may come from the other side on which an unknown, running against the hero and against the tide, still managed to gain a respectably large vote. And he did that without a big public relations ballyhoo.

The two most remarkable appearances of that campaign, an acceptance speech and a concession of defeat, were made without benefit of advertising. No format was tested at an agency, no gimmicks were devised for audience effect. There were no make-up men to arrange each eyebrow, no production men to supervise the camera angles, no charts to tell the audience when to laugh or cry. The words that were spoken were the speaker's own and the feelings that he evoked were the audience's own, for there is no public relations that can take the place of the honest words of an honest man.

Our Sins Are Your Fault

October 21, 1954

DEMOCRATIC National Committeeman Chairman Stephen A. Mitchell's thoughts about campaign ethics, as quoted in the New York *Herald Tribune*, have a worthy, if familiar, ring to them: Let's talk sense, let's not promise easy and painless solutions, let's be honest about our opponents, and let's put America ahead of party. But the same week these sterling recommendations were published, Mr. Mitchell dropped hints about President Eisenhower and Bobby Jones: their friendship, their golf, the propinquity of their Georgia cabins, and their respective relationships to the Dixon-Yates "deal."

A certain contradiction between Mr. Mitchell's code and some of his acts may be explained by a revealing paragraph he added to his statement about campaign morality. He said the Democratic Party ". . . cannot adopt a code of ethics unilaterally. If the Republican Party continues to use charges of treason as its campaign stock-in-trade, then the Democratic Party may be obliged to employ harsher words than we would otherwise select. It is not possible for one side to follow the Marquis of Queensberry Rules if the other side uses brass knuckles and an occasional kick to the groin."

This approach has the immense advantage, for Democrats like Mr. Mitchell and me, of blaming our opponents beforehand for any dubious practices of which our own party may subsequently be guilty. Whatever we may do, it's their fault, because they started it. Here is our Democratic contribution to that political ethic, currently popular in many quarters, which holds that the present company is by definition righteous and therefore all its sins should be visited upon its opponents.

A classic recent example of this "our sins are your fault" doctrine is the embarrassed explanation of McCarthyism by Henry Luce and other conservatives that it is really the fault of the liberals — or, as they would probably say, the "liberals." The Communists of course explain that their measures are made necessary by the vicious resistance of bourgeois and fascist elements. McCarthyites, in turn, excuse their "vigorous" tactics by citing the unqualified evil of their opponents, the Communists and "Communist thinkers." And the Eisenhower Republicans complete the circle by blaming McCarthyism on Democratic laxity. Vice-President Nixon earnestly explains that Republican failures in Indochina are the result of what Democrats had done in previous administrations. And now Chairman Mitchell says that we Democrats can hit below the belt because the G.O.P. did it first.

Meanwhile, back at the ranch house, an organization called the Fair Campaign Practices Committee, Inc., has drawn up a code of fair play for the Congressional campaign, renouncing all sorts of nastiness. Stephen Mitchell has signed it, and his Republican opposite number, Leonard Hall, has signed it, too. But the remarks of the party chairmen as they signed, and their earlier articles in the *Herald Tribune,* make plain the deficiencies of such a commitment to virtue in general: Each party treats such a code chiefly as an enunciation of the deathless ideals which it has always exemplified, to which its opponents must now conform.

Mr. Mitchell's article cites Adlai Stevenson as the high standard by which politicians should be judged, and makes it plain in his examples that it is the Republicans who have fallen short. He did have the grace to say, when he took the pledge, that there were sinners on both sides, but he does not indicate of what specific sins on his own side he is now repenting. Mr. Hall would not even go that far; he simply called it a reaffirmation of a position that the Republican Party had already taken.

The code puts the signers on record against "unfounded accusations" "which aim at creating or exploiting doubts . . ." as to an opponent's "loyalty and patriotism." But what seems "unfounded" and "without justification" to us Democrats is apparently somehow justifiable to Republican consciences, and that's the catch. Different interests and different political positions appear with — and help to make — different definitions of words, different indices of importance, and different tests of truth. The rules for campaigns are not laid down by a Marquis of Queensberry and enforced by a referee; they are conceived and interpreted by the participating fighters out of the respective social philosophies which differ enough to make them antagonists. To each party it regularly appears that its opponent is not only taking wrong positions on the real issues but is also talking about the wrong issues. The area in which we agree about the morality of specific cases in our own campaigns is relatively small compared to the larger area in which what seems to be serious, right, true, and necessary to us appears dastardly to them, and vice versa. Therefore Mr. Mitchell's doctrine, that when our opponents do not abide by our understanding of rules we can break them, gives us a very handy latitude.

Take "corruption," for example. Mr. Mitchell and the rest of us Democrats have vivid and unpleasant memories of the sweeping attack in the 1952 campaign. The Republicans used some kind of special vision to discern a Great Pattern of Democratic Corruption which went far beyond the proven cases.

The same special vision now enables them, when they visit Washington, to see something they call a "higher moral tone" in that city, evoking images of a well-scrubbed, buttoned-up citizenry, in bed by nine each night, and up to read the lesson for the day before breakfast. But the discernment of these "tones" and "patterns," higher and lower, seems to depend in striking measure upon the prior conviction of the person discerning them.

Mr. Mitchell seems now to propose that we Democrats look for, or invent, some "patterns" of our own. When the public is given thereby still further encouragement in the easy belief that politics is a web of evil, we can always say the Republicans started it. When our cry of "corruption" ironically helps to make more corruption by the contempt for government it creates, we can always say they used the brass knuckles first. But even so, there are difficulties. For what if we should be returned to office? Then we would have to deal with the demons raised by our own campaign, as the Republicans are still learning after the campaign of 1952.

Let's consider the Dixon-Yates proposition. The reasons we oppose it have really nothing to do with golf, Georgia cabins, or Bobby Jones; they have to do with atomic energy, public power, and the TVA, and possibly with the way contracts are awarded. Our attack is important, and needs to be pressed vigorously and directed straight at the President, who is responsible. But if we win not on our own ground but through some unproved speculation about "corruption," what should we do the next time a public power and atomic energy issue comes up? Find another Presidential golfing partner?

These doubts are easier, I know, for an ordinary Democrat like me to entertain than for hard-pressed party leaders. They remember that when Democratic Senators tried hard to get public attention for the substance of this crucial issue, they were just accused of filibustering. Mr. Mitchell's charge, some say, gave the issue the "lift" it needed. But that "lift" seems suspiciously like the "lift" Mr. Eisenhower's "I shall go to Korea" speech gave to another complex issue, an imaginative statement that catches the public fancy but falsifies the real choices to be made.

Perhaps Mr. Mitchell's advice explains another recent move of the Democrats — the action in the Senate on August 12 to outlaw the Communist Party, or something. This move provoked great editorial indignation and the widespread and inevitable use of those well-worn quotation marks around the word "liberal," sometimes coupled with "so-called."

On the face of it it is hard to escape the conclusion of those editorials that the move did not help and may have hurt the causes of both anti-Communism and civil liberties. Some serious defenders of civil liberties and responsible opponents of Communism are said to have argued that outlawing the Party would help on both counts. But if the Democratic Senators had these arguments in mind, why did they not present them in debate? If the Senators were geniunely convinced that this was a needed law, why did they not explain in detail why it was needed, and why it was needed now? Presenting the bill suddenly, without hearings, at the end of the session, in an election year, in a form that had been drawn up, we are told, between midnight and one o'clock the night before, suggests that there was a good deal of cynicism in it.

Reading the presentation by the Democrats of their bill does not dispel this impression. Instead of offering careful arguments to explain why this bill was needed to attack Communism and to preserve civil liberties, the Democrats and the lone Independent in the Senate did these things:

First, they gave a series of routine denunciations of Communism.

Second, they used about every known cliché for going to the center of the problem. Hubert Humphrey, the leader, condemned "piecemeal attempts" and "working on the fringes and on the flanks of the problem" and "the rash of little resolutions"; he wanted to "get at the root of the evil" and at "the heart of it" and at "the center of the problem." "Meet the Communist issue in this country head on," said Senator Morse. "Join issue," said Senator Humphrey. "Come to grips" with it, said Senator Humphrey. "In no uncertain terms," said Senator Morse. Engage in "an honest and undisguised frontal attack," said Senator Lehman. "A frank approach," said Senator Humphrey; "Come clean," he said. Stop "fanning of the breeze," said Senator Morse. "Quit horsing around," said Senator Humphrey.

But in all this they did not explain how their frank, honest, undisguised, frontal, head-on, issue-joining bill really would get at the core, heart, center, and root of the problem.

Third, they gave what Senator John Sherman Cooper of Kentucky, who seemed to be one of the coolest heads challenging the Democratic move, called the "stand up and be counted" argument. "The issue is drawn," said Senator Humphrey. "Fish or cut bait," said Senator Morse. "They cannot duck this one," said Senator Humphrey.

As Senator Cooper observed, this argument shouldn't really count for much in a Senate of which each member could be presumed already to be registered against Communism. But Senator Humphrey and his colleagues seem to have their eyes on a different reality than Senator Cooper — not on the substance of our anti-Communist program but on the clamor of partisan charges.

"I am tired of reading headlines about being 'soft' toward Communism," said Senator Humphrey. "I am tired of reading headlines about being a leftist, and about others being leftist." "I will not be lukewarm," he said. "I do not intend to be a half patriot."

Senator Humphrey and his colleagues chose to demonstrate their full patriotism to the headline writers by proposing a bill in which it is doubtful that many of them themselves really believed. Their excuse is plain. It is Mr. Mitchell's: the Republicans used brass knuckles and yelled "treason," so we have to fight back as we can.

But if we meet the arguments of our opponents not on grounds of our own responsible conviction but on grounds they have selected to suit the mood of the times, then whose is the victory? From here it seems that we should meet the challenge of being "corrupt" or "soft" toward Communism directly, with such admissions of failure as are justified and with sharp replies to false charges. If instead we charge what we know is not so and propose what we do not really want, then we will feed the furies we should combat.

Just as McCarthyism is chiefly the responsibility of McCarthy and his defenders, and Communist tyranny is primarily the fault not of the Czars or fascists or capitalism but the Communists, and Republican policy is mostly to be blamed on Republicans, so we Democrats must bear the responsibility for our own acts.

The Debating Career
of Richard M. Nixon

April 19, 1956

RICHARD MILHOUS NIXON is an able young politician who has got himself into an awkward and unpromising situation — except, of course, that he may at any moment become President of the United States. The talents that have brought him to this powerful position may some day undo him.

The chief of these talents is his ability in the art of public persuasion. If Adlai Stevenson is the high-minded commencement speaker in politics and Dwight Eisenhower the morale-building football coach, then Mr. Nixon is the bright young debator. Almost his whole life has been spent in the arguing business, and his success has been, in the language of his native Southern California, supercolossal.

He engaged in his first debate, on the subject "Resolved: that insects are more beneficial than harmful," in the seventh grade. He won. In his California high schools he entered something called the Constitutional Oratorical Contest three times; three times he won. He led winning debating teams both in high school and in Whittier College, and when he entered the Southern California Intercollegiate Extemporaneous Speaking Contest, he won that.

In 1946, the Congressman in California's twelfth district, a well-liked Democrat named Jerry Voorhis, agreed one day to meet his young, unknown Republican opponent, Richard

Nixon, in a series of five debates. The first one was held in a high school in South Pasadena, and after it was over Voorhis asked a friend how the debate had gone. "Jerry," said the friend, "he murdered you."

Four years later, in 1950, Congressman Nixon was running for the Senate against Helen Gahagan Douglas, and a leading California Democrat spoke for Mrs. Douglas in a debate with Nixon. "He knew every detail," says this Democrat. "The audience was with him, and he made a monkey out of me."

Two years later, in 1952, Senator Nixon was running for the Vice-Presidency. "I come before you," he said earnestly one memorable night in late September, ". . . as a man whose honesty and integrity have been questioned. . . ." After the telecast, telegrams, letters, postcards, and even gifts of money came in by the thousands.

Two years after that, in 1954, Vice-President Nixon traveled across the country in a campaign expedition that, in sheer expenditure of lung power, is probably unmatched by any in the history of American off-year elections. The President praised him; everybody credited him with Democratic scalps; midwestern party chairmen publicly thanked him for what he had done "for the American people and his party"; and a Republican columnist voiced the conclusion of many when he said, "Virtually singlehanded, he averted a G.O.P. debacle."

Now, in 1956, just ten years from the time he entered politics, Mr. Nixon has talked and argued and campaigned his way to the threshold of the most powerful office in the world. As one of the so-called "committee of 100" that first picked Nixon to run in 1946, has said, "I guess we didn't know what we had hold of. We knew Dick was smart and we knew he could talk, but we didn't know that he was that smart or could talk that fast."

❋

For all the Vice-President's ability to persuade, there still are many Americans who remain quite unpersuaded about the man himself. The Democrats, who feel a special hostility to Mr. Nixon, say things like: "He doesn't give a damn about the truth"; "He's absolutely ruthless"; and "He doesn't have a shred of character."

The degree of opposition from one's enemies can be important to a politician, particularly when he is approaching the highest national office. Americans are not so neatly divided into parties that the deeply felt opinion of one group has no effect on the other.

Moreover, the strength of feeling against a political figure helps determine the power his opposition can mount against him. Many Democrats really like Mr. Eisenhower, and cannot get terribly excited about opposing him; therefore, he spikes the Democratic guns. Mr. Nixon's effect, however, is the opposite; he loads them. Against him the Democrats would unite and fight and work and give and organize and vote with a passionate response beyond that evoked by any other candidate. As one Democrat said, "If I think he may become President, I'll be really frightened. I don't mean just politically frightened, I mean *really* frightened about what it would mean for the country."

On most ordinary counts, Mr. Nixon does not appear to deserve this hostility. Personally, those who know him say he is a nice fellow. His social philosophy contains nothing extreme enough to scare anyone very badly; it is, in fact, a little hard to know what his philosophy is, but that's no crime or novelty amidst the pragmatism of American politics. His voting record is a mixed and mildly conservative Republican one; it has to be carefully edited by the liberals who oppose him when they want to make it seem to be something fierce. He "does his homework" better than many members of the Administration. His role in the Hiss case may not be quite heroic enough to justify the implication one sometimes discerns in his promotional literature, that a grateful nation should ever after do whatever he recommends, but still it is impressive. He appears in the record as an alert, intelligent, and persevering investigator. After becoming Vice-President he made a ceremonial trip to Asian countries that was considered a distinct success. It is repeatedly said that he has brought a new significance to the Vice-Presidential office.

One can find, from the calm between the storms of Mr. Nixon's campaigning, some quotations from his speeches that contrast with the usual list. He once admitted, with a little surprised aside noting that he was admitting it, that there had been great Presidents from both parties. In the fall of 1953 he chose to say in a St. Louis speech to the American Legion: ". . . let's recognize right now that the decision to go into Korea was right . . . on this issue President Truman was right, and he deserves credit for making that decision . . ." He also has said that "No party has a monopoly on patriotism or love of country."

Why then is there such a widespread distaste for Mr. Nixon?

To understand the feeling against Mr. Nixon one must turn not to the substance of his politics but to the character of his polemic.

Though the early ones are now many years gone, none of Mr. Nixon's campaigns has been forgotten; each has left a memorable stain.

For all their victories and acclaim, the champions in the art of persuasion, from the days of the sophists to our own, have been under a bit of a shadow. After the applause has died down and a more reflective mood has set in, one is never sure just where conviction ended and sheer artistry began. In our time these ancient doubts have taken on a new dimension, as the persuasion of men in the mass has become not just an art but a science. Mr. Nixon, in the practice of that science, has gathered not only laurels but also the antagonism that men feel toward its more unrestrained practitioners.

Almost everybody has been made to look the fool by a glib debater, or been sold something he didn't want by a fast-talking salesman, or been put in the wrong before a crowd by the "sincere" and emotional appeal of an opponent. Such experiences are remembered when one listens to Richard Nixon.

Mr. Nixon's success has been extravagantly admired. His friend and campaign manager, Murray Chotiner, who is credited with developing many of the Nixon techniques, has been sent on a tour to tell Republicans how it is done. Mr. Nixon himself has given lectures on the subject, with such advice as: "If he asks you where you stand on Dulles, ask him where he stands on Acheson. If he asks you how you stand on the McCarthy issue, make him say where he stands on Mitchell and Bobby Jones, on Roosevelt and Condon. . . ." But, in the long run, men are not satisfied with the technique of attack and counterattack, or convinced just by success; at the last, they *do* want to know where one stands. With Mr. Nixon, it is not easy to tell.

It is not that he hasn't taken positions; it is just that his arguing and persuading and his platform performances are much more central to his public personality than any clear political commitment; his articulate ability to sway a crowd is far more noticeable than any restraining set of values. The worthy things he may do or say appear to be, as in one of the devices that he uses in his campaigning, just the preliminary concession to truth or to the other side that one makes in order to win the audience, so that the final, calculated argument will be the more damning. It may just be a part of what you have to do to win.

The Vice-President and his supporters have quite different explanations of the feeling against him. Nixon's own version came out clearly in the unguarded moment just after the Nixon Fund story broke, and for some citizens the way he responded to the whole affair was more damning than anything about the Fund itself: "Hold the train! You folks know the work that I did investigating the Communists in the United States [applause] . . . After I received the nomination for the Vice-Presidency, I want you folks to know — and I'm going to reveal it today for the first time — I was warned that if I continued to attack the Communists and crooks in the government that they would continue to smear me . . ." An essential part of Mr. Nixon's presentations is to present those who oppose him as an assortment of evil types — Communists, left-wingers, crooks — while his own resistance to them on the side of good is cast in the most personal and dramatic terms.

The current biography entitled, with admirable succinctness, *Nixon,* and written by the subject's friend, Ralph de Toledano, is a longer and more sophisticated development of that same heroic, good guy–bad guys theme. This sympathetic biography of him is composed in large part of attacks on his critics.

Sometimes this attack proceeds from very dark assumptions; Toledano says that "Nixon is hated most by those who most hate themselves." This strange item of high psychology is just tossed off in passing and not explained. But the main thrust of his argument is that his admired subject is disliked by left-wing intellectuals because, in two instances, the Nixon Fund and the Hiss case, he showed them to be wrong.

The Fund matter, however, was hardly a case of showing "intellectuals" to be "wrong"; it may have been a case of showing them to be in the minority, but that is hardly the same thing. It is interesting that Mr. Nixon's biographer should not notice the distinction, and, apparently like his subject, should conclude that right and wrong are determined by Hooper ratings.

The questions raised by the Fund were not answered in the famous telecast, but were smothered in references to cloth coats, St. Patrick's Day, and Alger Hiss, and by elaborate details of the Nixon family finances. From the television speech and subsequent information about Mr. Nixon, a reader comes to feel he knows the Nixon's financial situation better than his own; there is even a little, faintly socialistic, complaint by Mrs. Nixon, possibly reflecting her background as a Democrat, about the prices that doctors charge the family now that its head is Vice-President. But all this is irrelevant; the question about the Fund, to paraphrase a distinction that Mr. Nixon made about Adlai Stevenson in 1952, does not have to do with Nixon's personal honesty, but with his *judgment:* He accepted a special fund from one segment of his constituency as a "salesman against socialism," and may thus have obligated himself to their ideological position. Amid all the dramatic, personal, and emotional details, that main question went unnoticed. Another debating device that can be learned from Mr. Nixon is that it is better to deal with an irrelevancy on which one can make an effective performance than with a relevant point on which one may be less compelling.

As to the Hiss case, the feeling of resentment that Mr. Toledano describes fastened much more on Whittaker Chambers than on Nixon. The doubts about Mr. Nixon began with the 1946 campaign before there *was* any Hiss case; they have

grown with the 1950, 1952, and 1954 campaigns without reference to that case. They exist among conservatives — one who
has felt them so deeply that he avoided contact with Mr. Nixon
after the 1954 election, and who said that Mr. Nixon's "name is
mud," is Speaker Sam Rayburn. They are pretty widespread.
The poll takers, when they were wondering if Mr. Nixon might
run for President, found him running behind either Stevenson
or Kefauver; Walter Davenport of *Collier's* recently crossed
the country asking people about politics, and reported thus:
"Nixon? The noes ran down the line like echoes. No Nixon.
Why? Too young. Too emotional. Too slick. Not enough
experience. Only now and then, from California to New
Hampshire, was I to find Nixon votes . . . Lacked stature. Just
another opportunist. Didn't look the part. Just another slick
politician."

The other characteristic of Mr. Nixon's public personality,
related to his debating, also bears both a secret of his rapid rise
to power and a possibility of his defeat: that is his ability to fit
any of the major factions of his party while being identified with
none. Even more than Mr. Eisenhower, he transcends the old,
still bitter Dewey-Taft split in the party — and even the division over McCarthy. He manages to keep in touch with all
sides of the party; he has been described by various commentators on his Vice-Presidency as "a bridge," "cement," and
"a broker" among the different factions; the *Reporter* once said
he was "all things to all Republicans." But whereas Mr. Eisenhower transcends the factions of his party by touching upon
simple, clear, often platitudinous values that all Americans
share, Mr. Nixon rises above the factions by emphasizing the
practical necessities that all Republicans share; where Mr.
Eisenhower comes close to finding the common denominator
for the country, Mr. Nixon finds the common denominator for

Republicans. That means most certainly the attack upon Democrats; on that all Republicans agree, and in that, he excels.

Mr. Nixon is thus perhaps deserving, as has been suggested, of Mr. Taft's old label, "Mr. Republican." On him, however, it would mean something quite different. Where Taft defined Republicanism by a distinct philosophy to which he tried manfully, though unsuccessfully, to get the party to conform; and where he looked on those "me-too" New Deal Republicans who did not hold to his orthodox position as some kind of alloy — not quite real Republicans — Mr. Nixon is not so demanding. He has no discernible policy requirements for Republicans; he takes the party as he finds it and makes the persuader's case for what is given. He argues for Clifford Case against conservative Republicans; he argues for Henry Dworshak against liberal Republicans; when he goes into Indiana after a bitter fight between Jenner's forces and those of Governor Craig, an Eisenhower supporter, he has glowing words of praise for Governor Craig — and also for Senator Jenner. He says to assembled party workers: "We've got to get forty-eight votes in the Senate and let's get that into our heads." It is not surprising that party chairmen really love him.

But the support he gets from Republicans concerned with policies and philosophies as well as partisan success is tempered with a note of wariness. A Taft Republican said: "I'm not sure that Nixon is as conservative as I would like, but when all the radicals began talking about dumping him, I was for him. I love him for the enemies he has made."

Nixon has combined the sides of the party not by a weak and compromising middle position, but by a sustained, vigorous attack that, waiving factional differences, concentrates on the common enemy.

Yet he can be very winning, as when, introduced by a fumble as "President Nixon," he turned the error aside with a modest little disclaimer; he can also be a little frightening, as when he had a man who called out one sentence of heckling during a television speech brought forward afterward, held while he lectured him in front of the crowd, and then thrown out of the hall. In any case, he is full of smiles, "sincere" passages, pauses in the right places ("his [Eisenhower's] strength and his wisdom [pause] — and his faith"), and audience contact: (Nixon: "He [Stevenson] makes speeches like Acheson. Do you want to promote Acheson to the Presidency . . . ?" Crowd: "No").

His campaigning also cannot be understood apart from the devices that accompany it. In 1946 there were telephone calls that Mr. Toledano tries now to say didn't exist, which said: "I know you will vote for Nixon, because Voorhis is a Communist."

In the 1954 campaign, Nixon's speeches in the West correlated with booklets on "Senator Murray and the Red Web Over Congress" and advertisements asking "How red is John Carroll?" A candidate cannot, of course, be held responsible for all that is done by his supporters, but in Mr. Nixon's case what was done has been on a very large scale, with billboards, full-page ads, expensive public relations firms, and fancy techniques, in very similar ways each time. It has always played on the same themes, helping create an atmosphere in which his meaning is understood.

Other Republicans have defeated Democratic opponents without incurring the special disapproval reserved for Mr. Nixon. Senator Knowland, for example, who represents positions at least as far removed from those of many Democrats, expresses them in a campaign in a quite different way: ". . . no Democratic Administration which follows the Truman Administration could divorce itself from the mistakes of the past seven years." Compare that stodgy, earthbound sentence with the higher flights of Richard Nixon on the same subject.

When Senator Richard Neuberger came to Washington, the

Oregon Democrat gave a speech at the women's press club, with Nixon present, in which he criticized those who violate the Ten Commandments in their campaigning. He pointed to Senator Knowland, who was also present, as an example of a man who had campaigned against him fairly. He didn't mention Mr. Nixon by name, and says that he didn't know he would be there, and was just saying what he had said and worked out long before. But everybody assumed he was attacking the Vice-President, and the wife of a Republican Senator left the meeting in protest. Senator Neuberger said, "Apparently the shoe fit."

Some Republicans know that the shoe fits. Back in 1950, Earl Warren did not support him for the Senate, and there have been strong Republican rumblings against him in California throughout his career. Some Eastern Republicans wonder about his appeal to the "independent vote." This expert at making others into "controversial figures" has himself become one. In a time when partisans are suspect and independents praised, he may be too thoroughly Republican for the good of the Republican Party.

The President is "liked" with an affection that rises above parties; the Vice-President is disliked with a hostility that also transcends political positions. Where the President has refused to use compound words built from a politician's name, such words ("Trumanism," or, as Nixon prefers, "discredited Trumanism") are a major feature of Mr. Nixon's vocabulary. Where the President has refused to "deal in personalities," personalities have been Mr. Nixon's stock-in-trade.

Most politicians, unlike Mr. Eisenhower, do — and in some cases probably should — specifically mention their opponents. Plenty of Republicans have called Democrats names, and plenty of Democrats have reciprocated. But Mr. Nixon's way of engaging in this autumn sport is his own. He does not say "Dean Acheson is a pink," or "spineless"; he speaks rather of "Acheson color blindness — a form of pinkeye — toward the Communist threat in the United States"; and of "Dean Acheson's spineless school of diplomacy which cost the free world six hundred million former allies in the past seven years of Trumanism." He does not say that Acheson and Stevenson are cowards or Communists or college intellectuals; rather he explains that Mr. Stevenson has a degree all right — a "Ph.D. from the Acheson college of Cowardly Communist Containment." Mr. Nixon's way is imaginative and deft. What does the word "cowardly" modify in that sentence? Just how does the word "Communist" fit in? He avoids a flat assertion that might offend some of even a sympathetic audience, but he achieves his desired effect and more by his careful phrase. That takes practice and planning.

Mr. Nixon's remarks are not, as with many blunt and adjectival campaigners, the crude, undisciplined, and exaggerated outpouring of outraged political emotions; they are rather the polished weapons of a skilled debater who knows exactly what he is doing, and who shapes his words primarily on the basis of a calculated strategy. There appears in Toledano's book, and again in a sympathetic article about Mr. Nixon in a Sunday magazine section, a remarkable little rule of thumb of his that is profoundly revealing: "The only time to lose your temper," he is quoted as saying, ". . . is when it's deliberate."

When you think about it, this premeditation, even about losing his temper, is a striking characteristic. Mr. Nixon has also said some interesting words about spontaneity. He told radio and television executives, in the fall of 1955, that candidates should make an intimate approach to the audience with a spontaneous, off-the-cuff speech. But, as the *Times* reported it, "An efficient 'off-the-cuff' appearance on television, creating the illusion of intimacy so desirable to win the viewers, according to Mr. Nixon, entails many hours of preparatory work." Mr. Nixon told about planning the spontaneous intimacy of his Fund speech. The broadcast was put off from Sunday night to Tuesday for two reasons: to give him time to prepare thoroughly, and to build up the audience. "We wanted to create suspense."

A political worker who has seen Mr. Nixon in action says this: Most good stump speakers have a kind of intuitive feel of their audience, so that they play by ear, trying out themes as they speak, sensing what gets a response and developing it. With Mr. Nixon, however, it is a matter not so much of intuitive rapport on the stump as of post-mortems, careful polls, and trial runs. It is more systematic, more a matter of calculation and testing. Mr. Nixon, as everybody says, works hard. He acknowledged in the early days of the 1952 campaign that his principal mission in barnstorming through Maine was to try out campaign techniques. One can see them developing — the scandal-a-day Administration, the "four-headed monster that was Korea, Communism, corruption, and controls," the boys dying in Korea while Mr. Stevenson makes jokes — and as Mr. Nixon gets the most effective phrases and themes worked out and polished, he then repeats them at each town. By the end of the campaign his speech has become a veritable masterpiece of planned spontaneity and deliberate loss of temper.

Some of his devices are traditional platform tricks: mock-serious "advice" to the opponent ("I would suggest to Mr. Stevenson . . ."); challenges to say whether he has stopped beating his wife (Will he continue the "blindness and ignorance toward Communism"?); thrusts to leave him with the burden of proof ("If that is not true, let them deny it"). Like everybody else, only more so, he uses metaphors ("Side-Saddle Adlai . . . his feet stick out to the left"), rhymes ("Morse . . . Well, he acts just like a horse"), and alliteration ("Korea, Communism, corruption, and controls"). His summaries of the differences between the parties can be breathtaking in their simplicity ("The Truman-Acheson policy got us into war; the Eisenhower-Dulles policy got us out").

Mr. Nixon also uses the device of counting on the ignorance of the audience and making a simple, memorable charge, the answering of which would involve the opponent in too complex an explanation to be grasped in a swift exchange. Against Representative Voorhis, for example, Nixon's forces claimed that Voorhis's colleagues in the House thought so little of him that they had passed only one of the 132 bills he had introduced, and that that one — here comes a laugh — was the "Rabbit Transfer Bill." This attack was infuriating to Congressmen who knew Mr. Voorhis as an exceptionally devoted and respected member of the House, but Mr. Voorhis' patient effort to explain the Rabbit Transfer Bill was not very effective.

In the Voorhis campaign one of the techniques more especially distinctive to Mr. Nixon began to appear, that of linkage. Mr. Nixon's experience in politics must have been disillusioning for a clean-cut American boy because everybody ho has ever campaigned against has turned out, on his investigation, to be linked to somebody sinister. It must be very sad for him never to have had an opponent he could really treat as honorable. Mr. Voorhis was linked to the National Citizens PAC, which in turn was linked to the CIO-PAC, which in turn was linked to outer darkness. Voorhis was not endorsed by the CIO, and was surely anti-Communist, but the whole linkage was handily foreshortened to "A vote for Nixon is a vote against the PAC [and] its Communist principles."

Against Mrs. Douglas, in addition to allowing himself to wonder out loud about the state of her health, Mr. Nixon worked out and used as a major theme of his campaign a linkage with Congressman Vito Marcantonio — he had learned, apparently, that it can be more powerful to use a particular individual. The way this one was done was to list the votes on which Mrs. Douglas and Marcantonio had voted on the same side, to parade the total number, hence to equate their political activity, and to ask "Would California send Vito Marcantonio to the United States Senate?"

In 1952, just after the Democratic Convention, other Republicans were a bit taken aback by the candidate the Democrats had nominated. But Mr. Nixon, with a brisk professional competence, went right to work to find the linkage for Mr. Stevenson. At first, with the "captive candidate" theme, he made the main link to Mr. Truman, with side links just in case: "He's Jack Kroll's candidate; he's Jake Arvey's candidate, and — this is his greatest handicap — he's Harry Truman's candidate." Later on in the campaign, however, Mr. Nixon was to work out a much more useful linkage for Mr. Stevenson, one that he had got plenty of mileage out of before, and one he used for all it was worth: Alger Hiss.

An interesting little subordinate motif in his attack on the Democratic candidate was the "mouse" theme. Many of Mr. Nixon's edifying metaphors come from the animal kingdom: Communists are rats, Morse is a horse, President Truman is braying about the country. In Binghamton, New York, he said Mr. Stevenson was a "waltzing mouse." In a speech in Joplin,

Missouri, he listed ten reasons why Mr. Stevenson was "unfit" to be President ("His soft attitude toward the Communist conspiracy at home as proven by his defense of Alger Hiss . . . His cheap opportunism, as demonstrated by his willingness to help Harry Truman scrawl nasty words about Dwight Eisenhower on any convenient back fence . . ."), and included among them this one: "his mouselike dependence on Harry Truman." In a speech in East St. Louis he gave the "black record" of Stevenson in Illinois, contrasted him with Eisenhower, and ended with these stirring words: "The choice that must be made is whether we want to select as President of the United States a man or a mouse!" As one of the newsmen who covered his trip reported, laconically, Mr. Nixon does *not* speak over the head of his audience.

Mr. Nixon's attacks have an intensely personal quality; other political figures call each other names, but usually just in the line of political duty, without overtones of real derogation of the other's character as a private citizen. Mr. Nixon's remarks, though, suggest that there is far more wrong with their target than just that he holds the wrong political position. For example, he has dwelt on the theme that Mr. Stevenson is "unfit" for the Presidency. In a speech wholly devoted to that subject, one reason was that his subject had a "character weakness that could prove fatal at this moment of history."

On the eve of the elections of 1954, Mr. Nixon issued a statement responding to a Stevenson speech in which he said: "Mr. Stevenson proved again that thirty-four million Democrats, Republicans, and Independents were right when they found him unfit to be President in 1952." That is an interesting interpretation of what voters were doing when they voted for the Republican candidates, a little insulting to all concerned. One would have thought that some of these thirty-four million decided that, as between two "fit" candidates, they preferred Mr. Eisenhower.

It is not just opposing candidates, but the whole of the opposing party, that, in Mr. Nixon's campaigning, is connected with a sinister set of images. (Mr. Nixon said he possesses a "secret memorandum" to California Communist Party leaders, directing them to "fight out the issues within the ranks of the Democratic Party.") A major and continuing effort in Mr. Nixon's public presentations has been to connect the Democratic Party with war, subversion, and darkness. As a man trained to the platform, he heads straight for those issues on which the deepest emotions can be aroused: the blood of "our boys" in Korea, and Communist spies in our government on the one side; peace, morality, innocence, and Eisenhower on the other — and all in the starkest terms. Part of this is done explicitly. But perhaps the more important part is done implicitly.

It is the essence of Mr. Nixon's method to say something without saying it. This can be done by a drumfire of adjectives and associations resolutely and incessantly connecting one's opponents with all that is bad and one's own side with all that is good. It is crucial that these associations be repeated and repeated, drumming them into the hearer's subconscious. In Mr. Nixon's lexicon, for example, Americans for Democratic Action — an organization about which it may be assumed that ninety percent of Mr. Nixon's audience really know nothing at all — is always a "clique"; the way it "ruled" the Democratic Convention in 1952 was always "ruthlessly." Here is a passage from Mr. Nixon that shows how it builds: "Stevenson's is a slave labor program hammered together by a union clique that wants to continue holding workingmen captive to their selfish whim." In one short sentence Mr. Stevenson is associated with

"slave labor," "hammered together," a "clique" (any organization on the other side from Mr. Nixon is a "clique"), "captive,"
and not just ordinary whims but "selfish" whims.

Here is another that throws in a little of the advertising
man's appeal to the testimony of unnamed experts: "Let me
speak tonight of Adlai the Appeaser, the man whose slavish
devotion [not just his ordinary devotion] to the dubious foreign policy of Truman and Acheson could bring on World War
III. This is not idle scare talk. Seasoned experts, men who
know, firmly believe the Truman Administration is writing the
ticket for another global war — which could well destroy the
world as we know it." In addition to endangering the world
as we know it, Mr. Stevenson and the Democrats are likened
to those who appeased Hitler: "What we are seeing now is a
tragic return to the gray days of 1938–39, when another dic-
tator was being appeased by another set of confused little men.
Remember Hitler? The apppeasers thought they could 'contain' him by giving him Czechoslovakia . . . It brought the
bloodiest war in the history of mankind."

Mr. Nixon said all this in a speech in Evansville, Indiana,
in which he gave his warm endorsement to Senator Jenner.
He explained about Adlai Stevenson's holding his Ph.D. from
Dean Acheson's college, and gave a list of Democratic foreign-
policy "failures," well covered with adjectives. "Saddled with
such a heritage of complete failure, even Superman himself
would fail. Few would call Adlai Stevenson a superman." Not
content with that, Mr. Nixon added that the Democrats' choice
was a "second-rate Presidential candidate."

The finesse in Mr. Nixon's work is sometimes lost on unap-
preciative souls like Harry Truman, who persists in thinking
that he was called a traitor when of course Mr. Nixon really

didn't say just that; sometimes it is lost upon a too unimaginative public and press also, and someone has to follow after Mr. Nixon to explain his work:

In Oil City, Pennsylvania, in 1952, Mr. Nixon said that Mr. Eisenhower would have only one test: "Is it good for America?" "Compare that," he said, "with Harry Truman, Harry Vaughan, RFC Dawson, O'Dwyer, and all the rest of these crooks and these incompetents." Reporters asked his press secretary, James Bassett, whether Mr. Nixon really meant to call the President of the United States a crook. Mr. Bassett reported back that Mr. Nixon meant that in the Administration around Mr. Truman there were crooks and incompetents, and that Mr. Truman was one of the incompetents.

In 1954, in Van Nuys, California, Mr. Nixon told about a "dangerous well-oiled scheme" with "plans for . . . socialized medicine, socialized housing, socialized agriculture, socialized water and power, and . . . atomic energy." "When the Eisenhower Administration came to Washington on January 20, 1953," he said, "we found in the files a blueprint for socializing America." His press officer said later that he was not referring to any specific documents in using the term "blueprint" but was just using figurative language to describe the philosophy and proposals of President Truman.

In 1954, Mr. Nixon said, in Minneapolis, Omaha, and many other cities, that "the Eisenhower Administration has kicked out the Communists and fellow travelers and security risks not by the hundreds but by the thousands." A press report said he gave this sentence very carefully. When Stephen Mitchell said that Nixon lied in claiming that Communists had been kicked out by the thousands, since only a handful of those who had been kicked out might conceivably be labeled as "subversive," Nixon's aides pointed to the words "security risks" which, including anyone against whom there was derogatory information of almost any kind, accounted for the thousands.

In February this year, the Vice-President in a Lincoln Day speech spoke of Republican accomplishments on civil rights, of the decision of the Supreme Court under a "Great Republican Chief Justice, Earl Warren." To the immediate indignation that he would make a partisan claim for a Supreme Court decision, his defender David Lawrence solemnly answered that there was an unquoted comma between the words "Republican" and "Chief," which separated the party designation from the office.

The niceties of punctuation and phraseology become very important when one is dealing in blueprints that turn out to be only figurative, crooks that turn out to be just incompetents, Communists that turn out to be just someone who went on a bat, and party accomplishments that just happen to have, incidentally put in their midst, a Supreme Court decision.

When a man has built his career this way, it is not surprising that many people do not relish the thought of his becoming President.

Postscript 1963

Mr. Nixon's decline was even more abrupt than his ascent. In the fall of 1960, he came within a whisker of winning the office of President of the United States; he almost attained the very peak of power — almost, but not quite. He missed by the narrowest of narrow margins, and then he slid rapidly back down out of power. Two years later, when he anticlimactically lost the election for Governor in California, he was dumped out into private citizenship. After a short time he abandoned California.

During this rapid descent one had occasionally a mild impulse to feel sympathy for him, but before it could develop he would do something to squelch it. He took his defeat in 1960 with apparent grace, but then he brought out a curiously defensive and self-conscious book called *My Six Crises*. One granted, relenting a little, that perhaps his 1960 campaign, even with its transparent appeal to the non-profanity of Eisenhower and its slogans, was not quite as "bad," in the way this article describes, as his previous campaigns had been; but then his campaign for Governor — with the recommendation of the death penalty for dope peddlers and much about Communism — brought back all of one's old distaste. After the California defeat there was a weird rambling press conference in which — among other things — Mr. Nixon attacked the press; the characteristics of the publicity-politician all seemed to have turned sour.

The turning point of his career would appear to have been, with a perfect ironic justice from the point of view of this article, the campaign "debates" of 1960.

Post-Postscript 1964

Maybe.

Part III

A Private History
of a Campaign That Failed *

YOU HAVE heard from a great many people who did some big political thing in the Eisenhower era; is it not fair and right that you listen a moment to one who started out to do something in it, but didn't?

A letter was forwarded to me in Denver in the early summer of 1956, and I promptly wrote and wired and phoned and underlined my affirmative answer. I took the Burlington Zephyr overnight to Chicago; bleary-eyed, I took a taxi to the Illinois Consolidated Trust Company Building at 231 South LaSalle Street; still accompanied by my suitcase, I took the elevator up to the eighth floor; and there, quickly meeting the Governor and other eminences, and then eagerly trying to write political prose before the day was out, I became connected with what may well be the most forgettable presidential campaign in recent American history. (Forgettable, that is, to the world at large. For myself, I remember it well, and loved it all, except for the losing.)

The 1956 Stevenson campaign was then at its high point of mere hopelessness, from which it was later to descend, with mistakes within and disasters without, down through varying stages of what Samuel Hoffenstein might call Fairly Utter Despair, into the final irrelevance, obscurity, and defeat.

* I borrowed the title, the opening, and the closing of this from Mark Twain; the rest I had to write myself, from notes made at the time, and from memories.

From the start, of course, Mr. Eisenhower's staggering popularity, well known perforce to the Stevenson people, had cast its benignly oppressive shadow over the whole effort. However, in the background there was also the unmentionable but possibly potent fact that Mr. Eisenhower had had a heart attack in the previous fall, and a stomach disease in the spring. ("This crazy campaign," said one of the staff in the dismal October that was to follow, "turns on two words nobody ever heard of before this year: strontium 90 and ileitis.") Mr. Eisenhower's illness and age, together with his unbeatable popularity, presented awkward questions of strategy, taste, and morals to the Stevenson Democrats (eager egghead volunteers kept having "ideas" about this, as about all things; one persistent screwball kept calling in his "idea," that there be launched a dramatic and very visible national campaign of sympathy for Mr. Eisenhower, called Operation Crocodile Tears, that would for his own health's good recommend his retirement). But the health issue, despite its unmentionable awkwardness, provided that miniscule element of doubt that allowed the Stevenson staff to hold in suspension its foreknowledge of the election's outcome.

As I arrived in Chicago, this disciplined repression of the human capacity to predict the future was in its most favorable period. On the second day I was there — the suitcase at the Morrison Hotel, the political prose cranking out of the typewriter — an Eminence put down the phone (he rarely did this, except occasionally to get a new number) and announced that Mr. Kefauver was conceding the long primary campaign and recommending that delegates pledged to him support Mr. Stevenson at the convention. Jubilation, Telegrams, and Cigars followed. Then Mr. Stevenson beat the remaining opponents, including Mr. Truman's candidate, Averell Harriman, at the convention. The afterglow of further Jubilation, Telegrams, and Cigars, the incalculable effect of the unmentionable presidential health, and some inextinguishable rosy spark in the human spirit, made it possible for the Stevenson people in that one brief August moment willfully not to let themselves know what of course in their hearts they did know: that in the end they would lose.

It is easy to say with hindsight (and it was easy to say with foresight, too, if one were disconnected from the thing) that the Stevenson campaign of that year should have aimed unequivocally at the higher reaches of Truth, Beauty, and Goodness, letting go all thought of Victory. It should have been a thing of beauty and a joy forever, one might say; it should have been American history's most inspiriting example of a candidate being Right rather than President. An eminent sociological writer made exactly that argument, in fact, at a lunch with two of the speech writers ("editorial and research staff") in the summer there in Chicago: Point one, you are going to lose; point two, therefore, do what you did in 1952, only more so. Since victory is clearly out of reach, Mr. Stevenson is free to say exactly what needs to be said. Talk sense to the People.

However sound this advice may appear to be in detachment and retrospect, it made the undetached and perversely hopeful advisees hop with fury. And one can construct an argument on their side. Can a major party's presidential campaign be mounted on the flat assumption that it will lose? The possibility of victory is of course an important psychological ingredient in the effort to achieve it; that is why candidates throw out those pseudo-stirring and often patently unbelievable statements about how We Are Going to Win and A Great Tide Is Moving Our Way and We Will Have a Great Victory

on November Fourth, et cetera. In the situation you almost
have to talk that nonsense to the people.

And the candidate is not a lonely writer, composing for the
anthologies; he is bound to all the candidates who share, often
rather uncomfortably, a place on the same ticket; and to all
the campaign workers and policies and partisan hopes that rise
and fall with him. For the man at the top to indulge his own
purely abstract intellectual and aesthetic and even moral convictions (without, that is, counting the obligation to try, along
with his — pardon the word — "team" to *win;* without attention to what his resolute personal sense-talking might do to the
votes, and hence to the party and to all the fellow Democrats
running underneath his name) would be irresponsible.

So the argument might go. Whether or not one finds it altogether convincing now, it had its force at the time. And such
rational arguments had irrational reinforcements. The politi-
cal-prose-typing self, flying on the wings of rhetoric, resists the
awareness that all those bold words will go for naught.

Then there was the matter of the 1952 Stevenson campaign.
Because that campaign had ended in defeat, it was systematically denounced and rejected, root and branch. That sociological writer, innocently analyzing things at lunch, could not have
touched on a more sensitive nerve than by praising the '52
campaign. In the Illinois Consolidated Trust Building, especially up in the separate rooms where the "editorial and research" people typed, phoned, and talked, it was dogma that
the 1952 campaign was a mistake: "Last time we tried the
eggheads; this time we try the people."

I encountered this dogma ill equipped. I *liked* the 1952
campaign. I brought with me to Chicago a very considerable
portion — five-eighths, let us say, or even two-thirds — of that
large and peculiar enthusiasm Mr. Stevenson had evoked in

me, as in thousands, in that 1952 campaign. But quickly I learned that, although enthusiasm for Mr. Stevenson was fine, enthusiasm for 1952 eggheadedness was not.

Remember that shock of recognition that spread through the campuses, and other such places, when Mr. Stevenson appeared on the national stage in 1952? Probably we all make political choices more on our fellow feelings, and our unfellow feelings, than civics teachers would advise; that 1952 election, especially, brought out notions of what persons and countries should be like, about systems of values and ideas of culture, that went far beyond the political matter-at-hand. Ike was EveryAmerican, and especially the practical-but-idealistic, successful-but-moral, eminent-but-friendly-and-unthreatening one, with whom the huge swath of middle-middle American-Americans could identify. Mr. Stevenson, in all too perfect contrast, was EveryOtherAmerican; he symbolized, up at this highest point of national attention and potential power, the other Americans who stayed home from the ball game.

No doubt that makes a sizable problem politically. The characteristics that intense supporters especially liked in Mr. Stevenson — the   seriousness-of-our-times-and-burden-bearing theme,   the   tell-them-what-they-need-to-hear-not-what-they-want-to-hear theme, the national and personal self-criticism, the allusions and taste and care about words, the resistance to clichés, the self-deprecatory humor and satirical wit — were all, almost by definition, prized by a minority, contrasting itself to the great majority and to the great main trend of the society. In a line whose business it is to win millions, that creates a difficulty.

The recommended 1956 way out of that difficulty seemed to be by total reversal. The editorial-and-research people, at least, seemed almost to say: Last time the Governor gave good speeches and lost; this time, if he gives bad speeches, he will win. (Except that they did not agree that the 1952 Stevenson speeches were as good as Stevenson fans thought they were; the conviction that those 1952 speeches were overrated was part of the anti-'52 outlook. And, apparently back in 1952 some material and ideas had come to the Governor from black-market sources, to the staff's discomfiture.)

But in 1956 — there was to be no black market, no "eloquence," no "burden-bearing" elevation, but only raw, red political meat. I remember two of the staff (winners between them of an impressive list of prizes for writing and scholarship) soberly congratulating each other on the excellence of this "applause line": "We're going to take the country away from General Motors and give it back to Joe Smith!"

Joe Smith, you may mercifully not remember, was the fictitious fellow in a little ruckus at the Republican convention of that summer; he became our Democratic symbol of the common man, until, in the middle of the campaign (and not at all too soon) he was retired. As to General Motors, that Giant has, for some reason, more negative symbolic power than other great American companies (I am sure their public relations people have expensive conferences to contemplate the significance of this); a last-minute inspiration from the writing staff made sure there were no General Motors cars in the official limousines of the Stevenson Labor Day parade.

One part of the no-nonsense, anti-'52 outlook seemed to be a new openness to the wizards of public relations and advertising. Many brave words and true had been spoken by us Stevenson folk against "Madison Avenue" and ballyhoo and selling politicians like cornflakes. It was a little startling then to an innocent Stevenson follower, being taken around on his very first morning at the headquarters in Chicago, to be brought

into a room where there were not only "electronic media" men
and "non-verbal media" men ("buttons and bows") but also
talk about Image. The chief of this outfit, after nodding succinctly to acknowledge the introduction, tried out this phrase
on me: "The Man From Libertyville Who Believes in Liberty
— how does that sound?" I was about to say how I thought
it sounded when my companion said it was fine, just fine. The
two of them went on to agree that Mr. Truman had gained
because he came from "Independence."

(Later on, that Libertyville line was to turn up in the draft
of the speech, and a piece of it in the actual speech, nominating Mr. Stevenson at the convention, given by Senator Ken-
nedy.)

I was put to work, in the first days, writing scripts for the
five-minute television shorts it had been decided the Governor
was going to do. I wrote those things like crazy. Reading over
the drafts now, in cold blood, seven years later, does make my
heart sink. However, I would maintain they are still speeches.
They are just terrible, that's all; nothing worse than that. They
did last five minutes, and they still used direct human speech,
not phony questions-and-answers or gimmicks, and they did
have ideas, such as they were ("And I say it's not juvenile delinquency; it's *national* delinquency"). They were not yet a
total capitulation to the more streamlined tools of the age.
What happened in the actual shorts that eventually were made
I couldn't say, since I didn't see the things. People who did
see them report, for example, seeing the Governor holding a
bag of groceries (rather uncomfortably, I understand, as though
to say "What the devil are these?") and talking about the
High Cost of Living. I can well imagine that these produc-
tions left something to be desired. One of the electronic media
men associated with this and other such ventures came up to

our office there in the early days in Chicago and argued against *all* speeches. They are passé, he said. Tests show that they exceed the audience's attention span. He said that what one wanted was something visual — or, at least, short, punchy, attention-holding colloquies, in place of speeches. What was needed, he said, was film from the Governor's early trip around the country, showing him vigorous, handshaking, smiling, surrounded by cheering crowds, one of the people himself. A picture of a kind of Harpo Marx campaign flashed into my mind as he talked: the Governor on film, embracing cows and patting children and chopping trees and greeting workingmen and being uneggheadedly common, smiling and waving and being healthy (perhaps he could do a sprint or two) all without a word, while some selected announcer's voice explained that this heroic fellow was going to overthrow General Motors in favor of Joe Smith.

To our stick-in-the-mud arguments in favor of actual speech and political content the TV man replied, "I hope you know what you're doing. You are losing your audience."

Much later in the campaign there even came a memorandum from Ernest Dichter, the "motivational research" man, telling what "depth polls" suggested for the Stevenson campaign. Mr. Dichter's suggestion to Mr. Stevenson seemed to be that he turn himself into Mr. Eisenhower. His picture of the revised Image for the Governor was of an avuncular, friendly, confidence-producing figure, likable but strong. Stevenson, he said, should create the feeling that "you can rely on Stevenson." "Adlai Stevenson must become a real person." "It is important for Mr. Stevenson to demonstrate through his action that he knows exactly what to do." He should "act like a physician who establishes his superiority and certainty by predicting . . ." etc., etc. Also Mr. Dichter wanted us to know that people in their depths were wondering, "What will I get out of voting for Stevenson?"

(I must be careful to add that, although this atrocity was circulated, there was no evidence that anybody at the highest level took it at all seriously.)

Mr. Stevenson "came across" poorly in his first nationally televised speech, from Harrisburg in mid-September, for reasons mostly of faulty technique; the teleprompter was screwy, or he didn't know how to use it, or something, and he had an earnest and preoccupied glassy-eyed stare off into the middle distance, trying to follow the thing; also, his timing wasn't right, and the tail of his speech was left in darkness. In a suite at the Sheraton-Park Hotel in Washington the campaign staff watched the television set in anticipation, support, hope, apprehension and misery. While penultimate paragraphs ran out the time, an Eminence moaned quietly about the thousands it all cost, per minute; when Mr. Stevenson mispronounced the word "elite," staff people looked at each other in efforts at mutual reassurance. That Harrisburg occasion increased, I think, the anxiety of the staff about the devices of modern mass publicity. There were other occasions like it.

Early in September, after the opening exercises were over, the whole outfit moved from Chicago to Washington. There we all had rooms in one wing of the Sheraton-Park, and our editorial-and-research bunch had an unmarked suite of offices in a Connecticut Avenue office building. The Stevenson-Kefauver headquarters was across the street, proclaiming itself by a big banner; the Democratic National Committee offices were listed on the board of a building around the corner; the Volunteers for Stevenson were visibly volunteering around on a lower floor of our building; but our group had no banners or listings, and used the back elevators, in mild efforts at security.

Part of the reason was, I think, that Mr. Stevenson was not supposed to have speech writers. Another part was that if we had contacts with the press it might be distracting for us and overly instructive for them. Also, certainly, it was desirable to keep the public, especially the egghead public with its endless flow of ideas, out of our hair.

Shortly after we arrived in Washington, James Reston of the *Times* wrote a column about the conflict within the Stevenson camp. He said the "pros" wanted a tough, realistic, expediential campaign but the "intellectuals" (then joining the campaign, he said) would now bring to it their "high level." This was a good column, and an interesting and reasonable point, but it did have the defect of being in error. As a matter of fact, nobody was stronger for tough "realistic" expediential populistic campaigning than the "intellectuals" of the staff, and nobody was more disdainful than they of the "elocutionary debauch," the "elevated speeches," the "burden-bearing theme" that the Stevenson fans wanted. These intellectuals were the source and strong supporters of the we-can-end-the-draft issue, for example, while the chief of the professional politicians did not know that that subject was to be talked about, and would have been against it. Some of these intellectuals also urged that price supports for hogs be endorsed in Iowa ("demagogic," said the Governor), and that Mr. Eisenhower be attacked for denying Sioux City its flood control project by vetoing a rivers-and-harbors bill ("Boy, am I going to watch the returns from Sioux City," said one of the artists of the possible), and that the Governor support arms for Israel (these were the weeks just before one Suez invasion) and that he speak for tariff protection for New England industry. ("Ah-ha!" I said to myself, happily, as one who had read those books about real-life politics and about how things aren't all black or white; "I know what these are: shades of grey!") The intellectuals were also the most fierce defenders of the theory that foreign policy should be avoided, since there was no "mileage" in it. Of a high-minded draft for a speech on those issues one said disdainfully that "it would convert all the Barbara Wards in the country." In a cab on the way to an airport another one had a fierce, fast argument with a prominent Democratic lady, as follows: She (indignantly): There must be more foreign policy. We can't ignore the great issues of our time. Next week let's have a series of three speeches telling what needs to be done in foreign policy. He (bluntly): No. None. People don't want to hear about it. The Republicans, with Ike, will win on those "great issues." Stay away from them. We are doing fine.

The disdain for egghead eloquence of 1952 had its most emphatic effect on the "language" and as constant discussions at the time put it, the "tone" and "elevation" of the campaign. Never has there been such talk about High Levels and Low Levels, High Tones and Low Tones, Statesmanship and "Demagogy." Having got off on the wrong foot, an un-Stevenson foot, the campaign throughout was skipping and hopping to try to get back in step with itself. The Governor, weary from the long primary campaign, in which he had dutifully flung his rhetoric after the aged vote in Florida, pulled in the direction of "independence," of "statesmanship," of "elevation"; so did many of his nonstaff friends and advisers of the elevated sort. However, they pulled against a stubborn and unelevated resistance, not so much from the chewed cigars as from Mr. Reston's friends, the "intellectuals," on the writing crew.

The effect on "language" is suggested by the way that word itself kept appearing: "Get some 'language' out of that draft over there; it has some good 'language' in it." For a speech in Harlem some "religious language" was asked for; "What kind?

Saying what?" "It doesn't matter." "Language" seemed to be
a formless and available stuff, a kind of all-purpose paste
around the office in several flavors, out of which rhetorical
goodies could be concocted.

The circumstances of the 1956 campaign, in contrast to those
of 1952, were undesirable for Mr. Stevenson: his novelty was
gone, and he had to be on the attack, and he had to go through
the long primary battle. Another of the undesirabilities was
just that it all *was* in contrast to 1952, and from that fact there
came a complicated set of aftertastes, double-backs, reactions,
and backwashes. Most of these involve the intellectual and/or
egghead, with whose perplexing situation in the fifties Mr.
Stevenson's career was of course altogether entangled.

One of the reactions, intensified as the years passed, was a
simple negative. If his characteristics precipitated a devoted
following, they also precipitated a devoted unfollowing: a
group that had a specific distaste for him and his kind. Each
of those characteristics his followers like, these other folk dislike: his criticism of the nation's condition, for example, and
his rhetoric, and the satirical, self-deprecatory humor ("Bob
Hope wisecracks" against Mr. Eisenhower's dignity) that
leaves a businesslike and straightforward sobersides blinking
in confusion and distaste. ("Does he mean it or doesn't he?
Does he Believe in Himself or doesn't he?") He could be
taken to represent, for his detractors, all that is wrong with
what they would probably call, if not something worse, the
"pseudo intellectual."

Meanwhile that reaction helped along another reaction, the
Stevenson egghead finding this "anti-intellectualism" to be one
of the main things wrong with the age, and imputing to Mr.
Stevenson, in the enthusiastic 1952 battle, a complete set of

the excellences — literary, intellectual, moral, and political —
that were felt to be under attack. It was inevitable then that
there would be, later on, some doubling back in turn from
that, since the egghead is continually critical by nature and
hence inclined to be a little fickle: there came afterthoughts,
qualifying the high '52 enthusiasm, and also mild disappoint-
ments (as in 1956), since Mr. Stevenson was still measured not
by ordinary standards but by the impossible expectations he
himself had evoked. And finally there was a small and especially critical and perhaps politically sophisticated group within
the Stevenson camp who backed away, in their own turn, from
all that "egghead ecstasy" of the ordinary Stevenson fan: I believe that makes them, if you follow me, anti-anti-anti-intellec-
tuals, or hardboiled eggheads, and if you really want to know
what happened in the '56 Stevenson campaign, look at them.

The biggest Stevenson issue, about ending H-Bomb tests,
however, was an exception to their general rule, about trying
the people. That one issue, I think, became Mr. Stevenson's
1956 grip on his former and his ideal self. In the discouraging
morass of this second campaign this one big thing, at least, he
could hold to. The stubborn rectitude and the desire to say
what people need to hear — an attractive part of his 1952
campaign — got lodged in 1956 on this one subject. He insisted upon speaking about it, even though many politicos were
telling him it was very unwise (he could never match Ike on
any military matter; people were afraid that his position meant
weakness against the Communists; it was too complicated to
explain in the frenzy of campaigning; it split his own party's
constituency). Nevertheless, he kept on with it, steadily talking about the H-Bomb, and steadily losing votes. Whatever
the strategic wisdom of the thing, there was no doubt about
its moral seriousness.

❋

Our precarious pseudo semiconfidence could be maintained, with a little work, throughout September, but after Mr. Eisenhower entered the political battle in October the maintaining of it became downright difficult. The very next day after the President began to campaign may serve as a sample.

The Stevenson crew went to New Jersey on that day. We had a motorcade from the Newark airport out to Morristown. We drove in our chartered buses through the lovely North Jersey countryside on a beautiful October day, surrounded by the changing color of the trees, the singing of birds, the green and deserted hills. Not a soul or a sign or a voter was anywhere to be seen; the great VOTE STEVENSON placard on the side of the bus wasted its fragrance on the country air. The sturdy little band that did appear when we reached the town looked like a sleepy, pleasant morning meeting on the green of a special club — the birdwatchers, maybe, or the hiking club — having their own little project while the great mass of citizens slept or worked. At Paterson and Passaic and Fairleigh Dickinson University, the crowds were slightly less discouraging — polite, and, although skimpy, apparently not without some actual Stevenson supporters (though of course calls would come up from the crowd, "I like Ike," to which Mr. Stevenson would reply, "I like him, too"). But then in Newark the crowd was especially disappointing. We had no ball park full of North Jersey Democrats, but rather a downtown park gathering, by which went hurrying the great five o'clock crowds on their way elsewhere; Mr. Stevenson's gathering resembled that of a soapbox orator, with his group of hecklers and doubters in the corner of the park. In the hotel in Jersey City the staff people commiserated with each other and were prepared for the worst in Jersey City itself.

But when Mr. Stevenson came out of that hotel a police car, waiting there in the street, suddenly boomed out over its loudspeaker (the police, it would appear, are well trained in Jersey City): "Here comes the next President of the United States — Adlai E. Stevenson." When we turned onto the main street of the town we found it crowded four-deep on each side, as far as the eye could see, and lighted by torches. This pleasing spectacle was given tone by heartwarming political signs ("Fifteenth Ward for Kenney and Stevenson"). True, the signs had a marked tendency to put Jersey City first things first — Mr. Kenney (the Mayor and boss) being featured more prominently than Mr. Stevenson, but still it was good, after the idyllic morning in the Jersey hills, to see some actual people.

The rally — which was the Hudson County campaign kickoff — was held in the auditorium of a grade school, which seemed a small place to have it. However, the effect achieved by using the small auditorium proved to be a genuine work of political art. The place, being small, was absolutely stuffed, and people flowed out through the lobbies and doorways into the street around, to which the discourse within was carried by mammoth loudspeakers. We were scarcely able to get inside ourselves.

The entertainment provided for this throng by no means consisted of Mr. Stevenson alone. He was but one item on a very long list. By my actual timing, as a matter of fact, the band (they had a band, and it greeted each speaker with a rousing march) played as many choruses, and the crowd waved its halloween noisemakers as long, for Mayor Kenney as for Mr. Stevenson — when indeed the latter was finally allowed to speak. Mr. Stevenson sat on the platform — his white handkerchief in his coat pocket — between Joseph Tumulty, the huge representative from the area, and Mayor Kenney. The Mayor of Union City spoke. Candidates for assorted local offices were introduced, and some of them spoke. Governor Meyner was introduced, with jokes about his being handsome and (then) single, and he spoke. Then Mr. Kenney. After waiting with tolerant condescension during the long band-playing, noisemaking display for himself he gave a gruff and pointed speech to the Jersey Democracy. The "thrust" of it, as we say — and never more appropriately than in this case — was that he wanted tons of votes and no excuses. "I'm not interested in alibis but results," he said. "When the going gets tough, it's time for the talk to get going." He added — it was really unnecessary for him to add it — "We're tough." He specified and praised, in a rough-hewn way, all the candidates down to and including the one for Coroner (all of whom had already been introduced and some of whom had spoken), with Mr. Stevenson sitting there behind him on the platform. Then finally Mr. Kenney did introduce, succinctly, the candidate for the President of the United States. He did it with these, perhaps, ambivalent words: "I introduce Adlai E. Stevenson, the greatest intellectual in the country."

The greatest intellectual in the country then came forward and made a few nice little introductory jokes — just slightly too sophisticated, but mildly successful, nonetheless. Then, however, he started his serious remarks. He said that President Eisenhower had given speeches on the day before at Cleveland and at Lexington, Kentucky, and "I hope you read them." The crowd did not quite know what to make of this incredible suggestion; after a moment's hesitation it decided, apparently, that this must be a sarcastic or ironical proposal, and laughed derisively — as though to say, "Oh, sure, we'll rush right out and get them." Mr. Stevenson then gave the material that had been prepared, on the run, during the day, starting with lurching conferences in the aisles of the plane going up to Newark, that was intended to provide the newspapers his answer to Mr. Eisenhower. A noncommittal silence greeted this, with the audience holding its noisemakers perhaps a little impatiently. Then, instead of giving the prepared material about public housing (itself not as effective a topic when one actually sat in the Jersey City grade school as it had seemed in the Washington office), Mr. Stevenson turned to foreign policy. The speaker and audience soon came to have, as it seemed to me, that rare and peculiar relationship, perfect cross-purposes. The most exact example of this that I ever saw was in the presidential primary in Nebraska in the spring of 1944. Wendell Willkie was arguing his moderate case to the very conservative Nebraska Republicans, and tried to say that Republicans should not simply condemn one hundred percent, absolutely everything that Roosevelt had done, but should be selective. The crowd, however, was not prepared for such subtlety. Every time Mr. Willkie mentioned this Republican inclination negatively, the crowd cheered for it positively. He sat down in frustration.

Mr. Stevenson's discussion of the great issues of world politics with the Hudson democracy had something of that character. I had to leave to catch a train in the middle of the meeting. I squeezed my way, with difficulty, back through the crowd and two exits and the crowded sidewalk and out, into the city, which proved to be deserted. The Democratic voters supporting Mr. Kenney had been gathered from the whole city into that grade school auditorium and the sidewalks and streets around it, leaving no one else in the town. In case a few strays should be left somewhere, however, the loudspeaker boomed the speeches out across the empty streets. As I walked through them on my way to the railroad station I heard Mr. Stevenson crying out that "North Africa is in flames." I felt I could almost hear the crowd responding: "Swell; let it burn!"

✻

The last two weeks of the campaign combined chaos at several levels in an interesting manner. Along with other kinds, there was emotional chaos. One part of the soul was rising and falling with immense world happenings; another part was falling steadily with campaign developments; and still another lowly personal part, underneath these, was moving steadily along that high plane of perverse pleasure that we can feel when we can participate in events that are full of life, even though they may be disastrous. Meanwhile, of course, the mechanics of daily life became a shambles; it was by no means clear in what city one's most recent toothbrush might be found.

When we picked up a paper on a late October evening and learned about the revolt in Poland, we felt two competing reactions: human sympathy and (hopefully subordinate to it) partisan dismay. From then on until the election there were, every day, such mixtures of emotions. After the Russians came back into Hungary, however, these did not include any high historical hopes, so the days were filled with overlapping miseries at the several levels, making great club sandwiches of disaster.

The world events furnished an unnerving backdrop to our own efforts. The Hungarian revolt was mixed with a discussion of whether Camden was the place to talk about small business ("I remember Camden last time, and they didn't look like small businessmen to me"); the Russian return to Budapest accompanied efforts to shape a New America position on duck-baiting (what is duck-baiting, by the way?); the Israeli invasion of Sinai coincided with a harried air trip to Boston, in which precious drafts of New America rhetoric were spilled out into the aisles of the plane.

Before we took that plane to Boston there had been a sudden and peculiar effort to make our Connecticut Avenue office efficient. A higher Eminence from New York arrived, incredibly, at that late moment, to straighten us out. While all about us were losing their heads, and some were blaming it on us, we were going steadily on to make the unrepentant minute yield its sixty seconds' worth of distance run. While the Hungarian revolt held the world's attention, and the Stevenson campaign was ever more clearly headed for a big defeat, and the main figures of that campaign were all out scurrying (with the train, seeking scientists' statements on the H-Bomb tests, raising money), meanwhile back in the office this sober effort directed itself to devising a new and better way to set forth on a single page the material the candidate would need at a whistle-stop. "I think maybe it's better if you just have a few key words in caps, and then the names and the data. Type it up once more that way."

When we joined the campaigners in Boston in the penultimate week, however, nothing could have been clearer than that the Governor's need for whistle-stop notes was over. Each development in the Suez crises sent complicated reactions boiling through the corridors of the hotel. The insane last days of a modern presidential campaign — beginning a paragraph in Baltimore, ending it in Philadelphia; a new metropolis every hour — were made more insane by major news developments every half hour. And through and around and over all this there was a constant intramural argument over the "H-Bomb issue."

When election eve came at last Mr. Kefauver, the vice-presidential candidate, who had apparently been lost shaking hands in one of the smallest of the small towns of the West, showed up on television, and paused for a sleepy moment while introducing his children as though he might not remember all their names. Mr. Stevenson wearily did make an embarrassing reference to the President's ill-health, and the 1956 Democratic presidential campaign settled awkwardly into its obscure place in history.

By that time I had recovered toothbrush and suitcase and was at home. I had not come to know much about high politics in the time of the Moral Crusade, but I had got part of it learned. I knew as much about how the losing looked as the man who invented losing.

Part IV

The "Religious Revival" and American Politics

THE PRESS says that the United States is having a religious revival now, but one wonders whether those are quite the words to describe what is going on. There is an increase in religious behavior, but it is not clear that this quantitative increase represents any qualitative change in the nation's religious life.

One might identify three different areas in which an increased interest in religion is manifest in contemporary United States: in the popular culture, in the religious institutions themselves, and in intellectual life.

One remarkable thing about the interest in religion among intellectuals is how separate it is from the revival in popular culture. The interest in Kafka and Kierkegaard, in Berdyaev, Maritain and religious existentialism, appears to bear little relation to the revival of religious interest in the broad mass of the people. One is struck by the lack of interest in the popular revival among the theologians, and the lack of intellectual leadership in the popular revival. There is no figure like a Jonathan Edwards of the Great Awakening, or a Walter Rauschenbusch of the Social Gospel period, who is at once a popular and a theological leader. Those who are most read and discussed among the intellectuals — Kafka and Kierkegaard, Tillich and Niebuhr — tend to be symbols of incomprehensibility and intellectual pretense to the popular religionists. Niebuhr and Tillich have a following, but perhaps more in academic circles than among the populace.

Meanwhile, one can speak of a somewhat separate renewal within the churches themselves. In 1940 less than half of the people in the United States were church members, today sixty percent are. Other indices, such as financial support, building for religious purposes, anticipation of religious activities, have all increased more than proportionately since 1940.

But a healthier sign is the lack of enthusiasm the church has shown for these statistics. Some of the popular religionists speak glowingly of a revival, but there is not much of this talk at the heart of the church itself. For example, the National Council of Churches, in a recent official statement, refused to say, as some members wanted to say, that there is a great revival in progress; instead, they said that this is a time in which there is a need and an opportunity for such a revival — which is quite a different statement.

But it is not of these theological and churchly aspects of the present picture that the press is speaking as much as it is of the "revival" closer to its heart — in popular culture. The chief leaders of this revival are Dr. Norman Vincent Peale, a New York Methodist preacher who writes euphoric self-help books giving a religious version of America's how-to-be-a-success literature; Bishop Fulton J. Sheen, a more theologically literate Catholic priest; and Billy Graham, a somewhat more traditional fundamentalist evangelist, adapted to modern press-agentry. All three have popular television and radio programs. Bishop Sheen's program, sponsored by a maker of television sets, successfully competes with a top television comedian. The whole "revival," in fact, is centered around, and partly given its form by, the modern media of mass communication. Religious themes are immensely popular with Hollywood. There is a flood of so-called Biblical spectacles, with Hedy Lamarr as Delilah, Rita Hayworth as Salome; and Cecil B. De Mille is busily parting the Red Sea and giving Moses a flaming love affair. These religious spectacles have, of course, been staple Hollywood fare throughout its history, but never in anything like the quantity of the present time. Religious novels, which also have been a staple of the American past, have now a renewed and expanded market: one out of ten books bought in the United States last year was a religious book, whatever that may mean. On the jukebox there is a new trend toward religious numbers in which religious symbols, phrases, and associations are built into the love lyrics. Editors of popular magazines show a new interest in articles dealing with religion; "faith" magazines devoted entirely to "religion" appear on the popular newsstands; popular magazines regularly feature articles on the lives of Dr. Peale and Billy Graham and Bishop Sheen. A *Reader's Digest* writer, Fulton Oursler, retold the Bible in modern *Reader's Digest* style in a syndicated newspaper serial with immense success. Studies report a continuing increase in the number of religious programs on television screens.

Religion in this manner tends to be compressed into the already arranged stereotypes and formulas of the mass media. It is "salable" religion, quite clearly and often quite candidly cut to fit the requirements of Hooper ratings, box offices, and newsstand sales. A large part of it is under commercial rather than churchly auspices. As salable religion it is entirely "helpful"; it does not challenge, offend or disturb, nor require effort of thought. It is "useful" in fulfilling already established nonreligious purposes.

The central theme of the popular revival is self-help. The

American emphasis upon the technical is here applied to the problems of spirit and soul. The religious writers, as they unabashedly and constantly explain, teach the "formulas," the "methods," the "secrets" by which the self may attain its desires. They do not suggest that religion might challenge the goals given the self by its environment; religion is rather a source of techniques by which these goals might be more effectively realized. The correlation between spiritually induced power and worldly success is complete. By practicing the right spiritual techniques, one achieves greater earnings, fame, and position — in a word, success. But even more prominent than outward success is inner harmony, "peace of mind." The best seller with that title, by a rabbi, has recently been topped by *Peace of Soul* written by Bishop Sheen.

Even more than "peace" this popular religious literature promises "power." The images of dynamic life, power, energy, vitality are constantly appearing as the goal of the self. By "spiritual" manipulation one is to achieve the force of life.

As with the self, so with the society: the popular religious revival sees religion as a help in achieving the goals of the nation. The current struggle is conceived as a war with "atheistic Communism" which, as Billy Graham says, would "pull God down from the skies." The struggle is often said to be between spiritual faith and "materialism." Religion, we are told, is our surest strength, our strongest resource. We need to have more faith because the Communists have so much of their very perverted kind; therefore, let us pile up some more religion in order to oppose the Communists more effectively. The "religion" pressed into the service of mass communication tends thus to be presented as instrumental to nonreligious purposes, and as unspecified and undifferentiated in itself. It is religion-in-general, or "spiritual values," and it is a Good

Thing. The possibility of idolatry, of false and bad religion, of the need to discriminate among the claims made on behalf of religion, rarely appears.

The popular religious revival is closely tied to a popular patriotism, of which it is the uncritical ally: religion and Americanism, God and country, Cross and flag. The two pieties combine in much public discourse, and often the American will slide unnoticing from one to the other. The broad religious revival has a considerable anti-Communist American patriotic component, and public affairs now has a notable component of religiosity.

There is in addition another connection between these phenomena, in the kind of politics that is prevalent. The popular revival takes themes of the American past, flattens and simplifies them; these become one source of a moralizing and pseudo-crusading evangelical politics.

The main characteristics of religion in the American past would be a voluntary, moral and active expression, more or less rejecting the social and objective forms of doctrine, sacrament and church authority. The central, free church tradition of American religion has emphasized, more than in other cultures, the conversion of the individual and the revival in the society.

From this has come a preference for crusading rather than political action. European observers may be baffled, and unpleasantly so, by the tendency of Americans to conceive their political activity and much of their other activity, too, in terms of "crusades." Especially now, at the height of this period of popular religiosity, there are crusades all across the country. In pursuing his great moral crusade, Mr. Eisenhower profited rather than lost from his not being a politician; his movement was helped by his presentation of it as something different — and higher — than politics. To the confused clamor of political relativities it is difficult to know what answer to give, but to a moral crusade the answer can be clear and pure. And the American religious heritage tends to produce men who want clear, pure answers, an unequivocal goodness which one can enthusiastically and wholeheartedly support.

It is not just contemporary Republicans who have learned that crusades are better than politics. The same emphasis has appeared in a social idealism which derives in part from the Protestant churches. The voluntarism of the American religious tradition when it deals with politics may tend to regard social problems as soluble if only there is a sufficiently enthusiastic decision of the individual and collective will. The moral emphasis in American religious tradition may tend, when it has become automatic, to be as moralistic about social as about individual problems, to regard it as most important that the self be kept pure from any involvement with unrighteousness. Compromise, diplomacy, the calculation of possibilities — the essence of political action — may be regarded as dubious and impure. Thus at the most recent national gathering of American Protestantism's official inter-denominational section dealing with international affairs, a popular midwestern minister, who had been evincing signs of disgust with the meeting, arose, strode dramatically to the front of the hall and said, "Why are we dealing with all of this power politics? The job of the church is to proclaim the moral ideal!"

The mood which this statement represents is one not only ill at ease with concrete details, but also dissatisfied with programs which do not have the ring of finality and unmixed idealism. The free church tradition may be especially prone to look too quickly for the moral in every situation, and too easily to overlook the technical and structural, the given facts to which the moral must be applied. Its politics is the politics of sermon endings, of dramatic, clear, ideal, isolated, uncomplex causes to which the believer can respond with a revival enthusiasm. It tends to prefer one-shot solutions to world problems, as Europeans are aware from its effect upon American foreign policy. Wars are fought for specific and absolute purposes — to put down Evil once and for all — and after that purpose has been achieved, the nation can return to its normal and proper course. The continuing involvements of history and politics are characteristically ignored. There is a kind of individualism and lack of historical sense which is unaware of the problematic and the unintended consequences of actions and of the imponderables in history. As a man can be converted, in a moment, so the world can be changed, by a crusade. The "illusion" of American omnipotence, that America can do whatever she wants to, is part of the same ethos which a conversionist and revivalist heritage helped to produce. In short, the American religious tradition is geared to arouse enthusiasm and passion, not to produce wisdom and patience; it is more at home with single, simple, moral choices, than with complex, continuing political problems.

Some Negative Thinking
about Norman Vincent Peale

January 13, 1955

I'VE BEEN thinking negative thoughts, which Dr. Norman Vincent Peale, America's most successful Protestant minister, says we should never think. What's worse, my negative thoughts have been about Dr. Peale himself.

Dr. Peale believes in the Power of Positive Thinking. He says "only positive thoughts get results." What results? you ask. Success, happiness, money, health, friends, relaxation, peace of mind, power, self-confidence, vacations on Waikiki Beach, and, what is to me a truly frightening prospect, "Constant energy."

The results Dr. Peale himself has achieved by following the "Magic Formula" of Positive Thinking are impressive indeed. His weekly network TV show "What's Your Trouble?" gets upwards of five thousand letters a week; his articles, such as the famous "Let the Church Speak Up for Capitalism" in the *Reader's Digest*, appear in popular magazines by the dozen; his own magazine, *Guideposts*, is one of the "fastest-growing inspirational publications in the country"; he himself has been the subject of many lyrical articles, including a cover story in *Newsweek* and "The Power of Norman Vincent Peale" in *McCall's*; his printed sermons ("How to Stop Being Tense,"

"No More Gloomy Thoughts") and his self-help booklets (*Spirit-Lifters, Thought-Conditioners*) are mailed around the world by his own publishing outlet, Sermon Publications, Inc., of Pawling, New York; he speaks regularly to large national gatherings, especially of business groups; he has a regular network radio show, "The Art of Living," and appears often on radio and TV in such special appearances as a one-night substitution for his Pawling neighbor, Lowell Thomas; Christmas cards bearing a cheery message from him are sold throughout the land; he has a weekly syndicated newspaper column carried "in nearly one hundred dailies"; and now he has a regular question-and-answer page in *Look*. Of the *Look* feature, the press release said, "Norman Vincent Peale will add new millions . . . to his already colossal audience . . . He will answer the questions of *Look* readers on social and moral problems. In his first article, Dr. Peale gives *Look* readers his advice on such problems as debt, falling in love with someone else's husband and the H-bomb."

Somewhere among all these activities Dr. Peale finds time to preach in the Marble Collegiate Church of New York City, where there are overflow crowds at two services each Sunday. The worship bulletins of the church dutifully record, in column after column, the far-flung enterprises of the minister, with dates, times, and prices. The "lounge" of the church serves as a salesroom: thirteen of Dr. Peale's sermons on LP records, $4.50; a subscription to *Guideposts*, $2; "maroon, gold-lettered binders" made to hold "a year's supply" of Dr. Peale's sermons, $3.

And then there is his book *The Power of Positive Thinking* (Prentice-Hall, $2.95). This product of Dr. Peale's constant energy has already sold nearly a million copies, and the publishers are said to have a goal of two million; it is available on records in an RCA album ("You can hear the inspiring talks of Dr. Norman Vincent Peale *right in your own home!*") and now there is an edition for young people ("Your market — every parent among the millions who have read this inspirational best seller . . . Specially rewritten by Dr. Peale and adapted to the needs and interests of young people . . . Backed by major national advertising, special juvenile market advertising, and all-out Christmas advertising"). For 112 weeks, as of this writing, *The Power of Positive Thinking* has been on the *Times'* best-seller list, a far longer time than any other current book, and for most of that time it has been the nonfiction leader. For 1954 it will undoubtedly duplicate its performance of 1953, when, according to Prentice-Hall, it sold more copies than any other book — fiction or nonfiction — except the Bible. It is now being readied, apparently, to pass that one last competitor, for a "new Deluxe Pocket Edition" ($3.95) has been placed on the market, "Bound handsomely in genuine Sturdite . . . stamped in gold with flexible binding . . . wrapped attractively in cellophane . . . ideal for carrying in pocket or purse . . . printed on fine white Bible paper."

I have just read *The Power of Positive Thinking*. In addition, I have read Dr. Peale's other books: *A Guide to Confident Living* ($2.95), *You Can Win* ($1.50), *The Art of Living* ($1.50), and those of which he is co-author, *Faith Is the Answer* ($2.95) and *The Art of Real Happiness* ($2.95). Let me say, in the unlikely event that anyone else would undertake this redundant inspirational feat, that it isn't necessary. If you have read one, you have read them all. There are no surprises in Dr. Peale. The chapters of his books could easily be transposed from the beginning to the middle, or from the end to the beginning, or from one book to another. The paragraphs could be shuffled and rearranged in any order. The swarms of examples, which alternate successful business executives and successful athletes, with successful military figures thrown in for variety, could be transposed to support one point or another interchangeably.

As a result of reading Dr. Peale's one point in every simple, easy book, chapter, and paragraph, I am so full of "confidence-concepts," "faith-attitudes," and "energy-producing thoughts," of "thought-conditioners" and "spirit-lifters," of "10 simple, workable rules," "8 practical formulas," "7 simple steps," "2 fifteen-minute formulas," and a "3 point program," of "proven secrets," "true stories," and "actual examples," of "healing words" ("tranquillity," "serenity") and "magic words" ("Faith Power Works Wonders"), so adept at "Imagineering" and "Mind-drainage" (also "grievance-drainage") that I have the Confidence, Faith, Vigor, Belief, Energy, Efficiency, and Power to write an article criticizing Dr. Peale. Believe me, Dr. Peale, without you I never could have done it.

"The secret of a better and more successful life," according to Dr. Peale, "is to cast out those old dead, unhealthy thoughts." "To make your mind healthy," says Dr. Peale, "you must feed it nourishing, wholesome thoughts." The trouble with a fellow like me, he claims, is that my "mind is literally saturated with apprehension, defeat thoughts, gloomy thoughts." But my problem is not only that I find that there are real things in the world about which we legitimately can be apprehensive, nega-tive, unhopeful, and even gloomy from time to time, but that one of the surest causes of such negative thinking, in me, is Dr. Peale's own kind of "Religion."

The key to the immense success of that "Religion" is its mes-sage. In this, Dr. Peale differs from other heroes of the current popular religious revival. In a way Dr. Peale is the rich man's Billy Graham, furnishing the successful and those who yearn

to be so something of the same excitement, direction, and reassurance with which Mr. Graham supplies his somewhat less
prosperous and more fundamentalist followers. But there is a
distinction. As Mr. Graham surely would admit, his own message is essentially similar to that of hundreds of other evange-
lists, past and present, rising from a fundamentalist background;
the key to Mr. Graham's special success is not in any distinctive
message but in his personality and his virtuosity as a performer.
But Dr. Peale's attraction lies somewhat less in personal charism
than in his constantly reiterated single theme. Mr. Graham's
success depends almost entirely upon his personal presence,
but Dr. Peale has been as successful with the written as with
the spoken word.

This is not to say that Dr. Peale's personality and speaking
ability are unimportant. He is an effective master of an audience, full of jokes and anecdotes, buoyant and confident. But
it is his message that explains his unique success. One comes
away from Billy Graham impressed not so much with anything
that has been said as with Billy Graham; from Dr. Peale, one
comes away with a vivid awareness of the one thing he said.
It is an idea that has made Dr. Peale.

The idea is that affirmative attitudes help to make their own
affirmations come true. Dr. Peale takes the obvious but partial
truth in this idea and builds it into an absolute law; he erects on
it a complete and infallible philosophy, psychology, and religion so that he can solve every problem just by denying it
really exists and promise that every wish can be fulfilled just
by "thinking" it: "Expect the Best and Get It"; "I don't believe
in defeat"; death is "not Death at all"; "Change your thoughts
and you change Everything."

This idea enables him to say exactly what his hearers want
to hear. He can say it constantly, confidently, simply, without

qualification and with the blessing of God. He need say nothing that might cut across his hearers' expectations, challenge the adequacy of their goals, or make demands of them. Instead, he can affirm and reaffirm that it is simple to be exactly what they want to be, to have exactly what they want to have.

Dr. Peale differs from other leaders of the popular religious revival. Someone like Bishop Fulton J. Sheen has obligations to Catholic dogmas that prevent him from fashioning his message entirely according to popular preference; Billy Graham, too, has some restraint upon him from the more or less fundamentalist gospel to which he is committed. But Dr. Peale is apparently free of obligation to any intellectual tradition or framework of interpretation antecedent to that which he works out to correspond exactly to the climate of opinion and desire in which he preaches.

Though I have said that Dr. Peale's books are all alike, yet there is this one qualification: The later books are worse. The earlier ones, in which Confident Living and Positive Thinking were plainly foreshadowed, nevertheless spoke the message in something nearer to the ordinary preacher's tones. The word was already self-help, but the voice was more like that of an ordinary liberal pastor, with his three points, usually in alliteration, with homely examples, some passages from the Bible, a rhetorical flight or two, a few quotes from Tennyson or Shakespeare, and some spaces through which a word greater than any words of the preacher might manage to make its way to some hearer. But in *The Power of Positive Thinking* such spaces are pretty well sealed; every quotation from the Bible is cut, clipped, and interpreted to make just Dr. Peale's point; the rhetoric of the sermon has been replaced by the short punchy sentences of the advertisement; the three points of the preacher have been supplanted by the Five Things You Can

Do of popular psychology; and Tennyson's place has been taken by Eddie Rickenbacker.

Dr. Peale is good at what he does. He has the ability — and the nerve — to fit his message precisely to the exacting requirements of mass popularity. His discoveries parallel those of the composers of singing commercials. For example, he extols, and assiduously practices, "repetitious emphasis." He is willing to use without flinching the most blatant appeals and to promise without stint. The advertisements of his book explain, with remarkable candor, the basis of its appeal: "ARE *YOU* MISSING THE LIFE OF SUCCESS? Norman Vincent Peale's great best seller . . . is GUARANTEED to bring it to you! Make people like you. . . . Increase your earnings . . ."

Like other success salesmen, Dr. Peale numbers his points and fixes them in the mind with memorable new words; his "formula" for solving problems through the power of prayer, for example, is "(1) PRAYERIZE, (2) PICTURIZE, (3) ACTUALIZE." He is careful to avoid the slightest hint of anything that would be definite, determinate, or different enough to offend anyone; and above all he requires not the slightest effort either to understand or to act upon his message. As Dr. Peale says elsewhere, "Don't doubt. Doubt closes the Power flow."

Dr. Peale's idea and his ability to present it might enable him to be popular in any place at any time, but it seems to work especially well in America now. The importance of studying Dr. Peale lies in what his enormous success means about our present situation in this country.

The American roots of Positive Thinking are not hard to find. They include most of those characteristics which observers are always identifying as typically American: our self-confidence and optimism, our worldly practicality, and our individualism and striving for success, concerned more with private career than public problems. They include, more particularly, that special combination of these characteristics which places its practical, individual confidence in the triumphant power of "mind" or "faith" over all external limits. This combination appears in the peculiarly American religion of Christian Science, in the "mind-cure" movement of the turn of the century, which William James discusses in *The Varieties of Religious Experience*, and in many a "mental science" type of religion since. What Dr. Peale has done is to take these themes, which represent much of what is sound and also much of what is not so sound in American life, and reduce them to a unity, stating them in their simplest, baldest, extremest form. What was sound has pretty well been lost in the process.

But Dr. Peale's statement of his simplified version of these old American themes may be extremely popular right now just because they no longer seem self-evident. His success may be partly explained, ironically, by the fact that we no longer automatically believe what he is saying; we need to be reassured. Disturbing events have intervened, and so we listen a bit desperately to this voice which insists, more confidently than ever, that what we always believed is still true and that things *will* turn out all right, they will, they will. Just write it on a card and repeat it ten times a day.

The optimism is no longer the healthy-minded kind, looking at life whole and seeing it good, but an optimism arranged by a very careful and very anxious selection of the particular bits and pieces of reality one is willing to acknowledge. It is not the response of an expanding epoch when failure, loneliness, death, war, taxes, and the limitations and fragmentariness of all human striving are naturally far from consciousness, but of an anxious time when they are all too present in consciousness and must be thrust aside with slogans and "formulas," assaulted

with clenched fists and gritted teeth, and battered down with
the insistence on the power of Positive Thinking.

The success striving is different, too. The Horatio Alger
type seems to have had a simple, clear confidence in getting
ahead by mastering a craft, by inventing something out in the
barn, or by doing an outstanding job as office boy. The Peale
fan has no such confidence and trusts less in such solid realities
as ability and work and talent than in the ritual repetition of
spirit lifters and thought conditioners written on cards and on
the determined refusal to think gloomy thoughts.

The "individualism" of the message is of that "personalized"
kind which, having lost a genuinely personal relation, tries now
to recapture it by contrivance, which thinks it overcomes
standardization by stamping the buyer's initials on the product,
or which, by adding "and I do mean YOU," pretends to be
speaking to an individual instead of to a microphone and a
Hooper rating. Dr. Peale's works are "personalized" with the
same insistent YOU the Uncle Sam on the recruiting poster
used, sternly pointing his finger at the YOU who is everybody
and nobody. The drugstore I went to this morning had a new
sign tacked to the screen door: "Norman Vincent Peale Solves
YOUR Personal Problems — in Look Magazine." *My* personal
problems? In *Look* Magazine? No, thank you.

The effort to regain by devices what cannot be regained by
devices is especially evident in Dr. Peale's "power," "energy,"
and "vitality." The feeling of the loss of those powers must be
very deep. Every chapter seems to promise "power": prayer
power, creative mind power, faith power. This "power" is not
control over the world so much as over oneself. That which
should be natural — vitality, vigor, animal energy — is here
the subject of "spiritual" manipulation. Human powers are not
evoked by revealing some true center of interest and excitement in the world outside, but are exhorted to rise by the

sheer mesmerism of "repetitious emphasis." There is no real *content* to Dr. Peale's preaching, in the sense of some vivid objective interest: a job to be done, a cause to be joined, a truth to be understood. The transaction is entirely within the reader. There is a complete absence of any really concretely interesting and exciting world, which might bring out the reader's vital responses (and overcome his boredom, which must be immense). There is no such world because to see it, to be interested and excited by it, and to respond to it would require effort, and Dr. Peale's "amazing results" never require any effort.

This is a striking difference between Dr. Peale's themes and those in the American heritage to which his are related: His optimism and practicality are "easy" and "simple." There is never the suggestion that hard work might be involved in achievement. There are no demands upon the reader. This is not the sturdy practical guide whose maxims have to do with the shoulder and the wheel, the nose and the grindstone; there is no pushing and grinding to be done.

The master motif is that of the formula. The promised results are to be achieved by the contrivances and devices that are spoken of on every page, the "methods," the "secrets," the "formulas," the "techniques" that flood through the books by the hundreds. All of them, of course, are "scientific." The Bible is scientific, in fact: It is ". . . a book which contains a system of formulas and techniques designed for the understanding and treatment of human nature. The laws are so precise and have been so often demonstrated . . . that religion may be said to form an exact science." Christianity is "a simple yet scientific system of successful living that works."

Many of Dr. Peale's techniques come from the famous and successful men with whom he is intimate. In Dr. Peale's books these men turn out to talk just like Dr. Peale. There is a con-

tinually recurring episode in the books that goes like this:
Peale meets Great Man; Peale humbly asks Great Man for his
secret (his formula, technique); Great Man tells Peale strikingly
Peale-like secret (formula, technique) upon which Peale then
expatiates. Something like this occurs in *The Power of Positive
Thinking* on page 105 ("dynamic man at the height of his
power" — secret is to repeat Mark 9:23), page 117 ("outstanding newspaper editor, an inspiring personality" — secret is card
in wallet with words to effect that successful man is successful), pages 150–151 (Howard Chandler Christy, artist —
secret is spending fifteen minutes filling mind full of God),
page 229 (a Member of Congress — secret is be relaxed), page
212 ("outstanding man in his line" — secret is don't think defeat), page 223 ("a famous businessman who handles important affairs and varied interests" — secret is quiet period in
living room with wife after breakfast).

Everything in this maze of formulas and techniques is "workable," even the teachings of Jesus. We are referred to "competent spiritual experts" and to Dr. Peale's own "How Cards."
Dr. Peale takes all of our worship of the practical and the technical unabashedly into the realm of the spirit. But nothing
much that could be called spiritual remains. In place of any
Holy of Holies there is the bathroom mirror, on which you
are to paste the latest slogan.

The social and political meaning of this message is clear in
its immense admiration of power figures and big names. These
admired persons are all successful in the most immediate and
worldly sense: military men like Douglas MacArthur, for
whose faith book Dr. Peale wrote an introduction, businessmen, and athletes. No serious writers or scholars or scientists
or reformers or artists, no thinkers or critics, no one whose life
enterprise has a different goal than "success."

"Executives" as a class are special favorites of Dr. Peale's.

As the comedian Henry Morgan once said of *The Power,* "This book isn't for me, I'm not an executive; nobody in this book but executives." What the book can mean to executives is made plain in this advertisement: "EXECUTIVES: Give this book to employees. It pays dividends!" The most unsettling part of this proposal is not just that this "religious" book is justified at the cash register ("It really pays off in dollars and cents!" says William A. Cole of Tom's River, New Jersey) but that the profits are obtained by the executive buying the book in lots to use on his employees, quieting their complaints, making them enthusiastic for their firm, and increasing sales. Sales- men are said to have "Renewed faith in what they sell and in their organization" (apparently regardless of what the product or the organization may be). The book brings "Greater effi- ciency from the *office staff.* Marked reductions in clock-watch- ing. . . ."

Positive Thinking also makes politics much easier and more efficient. In 1952 Dr. Peale proposed a "prayer plan" to select the President, a plan which seemed to encourage its users to regard their choice as an absolute and divinely inspired selec- tion of *the* man God wanted.

God seems regularly to answer Dr. Peale's own prayers with the Republican candidates. He wrote a letter to ministers in New York State suggesting that they support Joe Hanley, the Republican candidate for Lieutenant Governor, because he had once been an ordained clergyman. In 1952 he said that though ordinarily ministers should stay out of politics, when there was a *moral* issue involved they should speak up, in this case for Eisenhower and Nixon.

About the current book there is a faintly blasphemous prom- ise, for a religious book, of a money-back guarantee. The mes- sage is endorsed throughout by satisfied users; it is PROVED, it has WORKED, it is TESTED. In fact, Dr. Peale's book is not much else than an extension of the advertisements of that same book, telling again between the covers, with further testimonials, what we have already been told, with testimonials, on the jacket and in the ads: This method WORKS. One might give prospective buyers of the book the tip that since the book is "repetitious emphasis" of positive thinking, one can achieve exactly the same effect — and save money — simply by reading and rereading the advertisements.

But to do that might be to miss what is beyond doubt the most remarkable of all the multitudinous examples of the power of Positive Thinking that appear in Dr. Peale's best seller, the incredible story of the Mustard Seed Remembrancers. For those who are too busy, or too negative, to read the book I now pass on this truly heartwarming story.

A couple named Flint were failing, broke, and full of negative thinking. They read a condensation of Dr. Peale's *A Guide to Confident Living*. The Flints, on reading Dr. Peale, were particularly impressed with the section on "Mustard Seed Faith." Though living in Philadelphia, they drove each Sunday to New York to hear Dr. Peale and continued to do so, says Dr. Peale, "even in the most inclement weather."

In an interview, Dr. Peale told Mr. Flint that if he would "utilize the technique of faith, all his problems could be solved."

One day Mr. Flint said to his wife that this powerful recommendation would be easier to follow if he had some tangible reminder of faith. They looked for a mustard seed. His wife fished something out of a pickle jar and he carried it around with him. But the seed was small and he lost it, and, since he had already begun to think positively, he got the idea that it might be put in a plastic ball. Mr. Flint asked Dr. Peale if he thought the resulting object could be merchandised, and after consulting a businessman ("one of the greatest executives in the country"), the gadgets went on sale in a department store in New York. The initial ad said: "symbol of faith — a genuine mustard seed enclosed in sparkling glass: makes a bracelet with real meaning." Dr. Peale adds, with the glint of Positive Thinking in his eye, "These articles sold like hot cakes."

The Flints now have a factory in a Midwestern city producing Mustard Seed Remembrancers, the perfect ending to the story of Positive Thinking. However, there is one unfortunate negative note at the end of Dr. Peale's account: "So popular and effective is it that others have copied it, but the Flint Mustard Seed Remembrancer is the original." That's the trouble with Positive Thinking; other Positive Thinkers come along and try to cut into your territory.

The Irony of Reinhold Niebuhr

January 13, 1955

THE MAGAZINE *Time*, with its way of making everything sound a little foolish, told its readers recently that "sin is back in fashion." This somewhat ambiguous announcement accompanied a picture, not of a new fall line in apples, serpents, and fig leaves, but of America's foremost theologian, Reinhold Niebuhr.

Time seems to like Niebuhr, and also to like the theological "fashion" for which he is the chief spokesman. But this Lucenthusiasm may demonstrate what Mr. Niebuhr himself might call the hazards and perils — possibly even the ambiguities and paradoxes — of success. For Mr. Niebuhr may find himself the victim of his own greatness, admired but misunderstood, praised but not followed. In fact, Mr. Niebuhr's whole position in America may be filled, appropriately enough, with irony.

Certainly the admiration of the Luce enterprises has its ironical aspects. *Time* and *Life* themselves provide excellent examples of much that Mr. Niebuhr criticizes.

Niebuhr warns against the cocky assurance that America is an innocent nation, and says we should remember the limits and the perils of our great power; *Life* speaks glowingly of "The American Century." Niebuhr indicts the comfortable who look upon their prosperity as evidence of their virtue and as an occasion for self-congratulation rather than grati- tude; *Life* lyrically extols the achievements of American capi- talism, with four-color pictures. Niebuhr counsels against extravagant estimates of man's ability to control history; *Time* and *Life* denounce the Democrats for losing China. Niebuhr finds inordinate drives in every man that make him capable of the misuse of power; *Time* and *Life* uncritically glorify Chiang Kai-shek and General MacArthur. Niebuhr is con- stantly attacking all forms of self-righteous moralism; *Life* says that if Stevenson is elected it will be by the vice rings of the big cities. Niebuhr says that history does not have its final meaning and fulfillment within itself; *Time* marches on.

The Luce publications are powerful representatives of a con- servatism which likes religion, which especially likes the doc- trine of original sin, and which sometimes seems to think it finds support in Niebuhr. A political scientist, E. V. Walter, writing about the "recrudescence" of conservatism, says that Niebuhr "has strangely been transformed into an inverted Condorcet for the 1950's," a pessimist for the conservative pres- ent corresponding to that optimist of the revolutionary past. But if Niebuhr is thought of in these terms, it is, as Walter says, by "a curious transvaluation and oversimplification." Niebuhr has often been misunderstood by liberals who like his politics but dislike his theology; he may now be misunder- stood by conservatives who like his theology but dislike his politics.

The evidence that Niebuhr is not to be found on the conser- vative side in daily politics is simply monumental. For thirty years he has poured forth an unending stream of articles to every conceivable journal on the non-Communist Left amount- ing, according to one student who tried to count them and kept finding ever new liberal magazines in which, sure enough, Niebuhr had written something, to over one thousand. He has participated in, helped to form, guided, or supported an uncountable number of organizations, movements, parties, and groups, including notably the A.D.A., its predecessor the U.D.A., and the Liberal Party in New York. He used to answer questions about his own political position by saying that the one sure thing was that he never voted Republican.

It may be said that "conservative" is to be understood in a more sophisticated sense, and that Niebuhr, whatever his own politics, has helped to create a conservative philosophy. Peter Viereck, a spokesman of the "new conservatism," admires Niebuhr deeply and says that his own attack on a fuzzy liberalism was partly set off by Niebuhr's brave statement on breaking his ties with the *Nation* to protest a fellow-traveling foreign policy. Francis Wilson, one of the new conservatives among political scientists, says he finds Niebuhr a stimulating alternative to the eighteenth-century presuppositions in much current political thought.

Niebuhr does provide something quite different from what we probably mean by "eighteenth-century presuppositions." He resists any tendency to think of history as controlled by laws like those of nature, and also any tendency to overestimate man's freedom to manage his own destiny; he sees the partiality and historical conditioning of all reasoning about society; he sees man's finitude as well as his freedom; and he points to the power of tradition, habit, and the organic continuities of social life.

But though these positions may often be seen more readily by the conservative, they are not in themselves so much a matter of conservativism as of the profundity of one's social understanding. The question is: Having recognized these stubborn facts, what then is one's position? The conservative gives one answer, Niebuhr gives another. The conservative takes the traditional and existing relationships not just as fact but also as norm; Niebuhr sees them as facts that must be taken into account in action that finds its norm elsewhere, in a Biblical understanding of justice. Niebuhr understands man and history realistically, not to discourage any challenge to the status quo but so that a challenge will be more effective.

The enthusiasm of the new American conservatism for Niebuhr's attack on liberal "illusions" is ironic because in American politics these illusions characterize both sides, and perhaps especially the conservative side. Niebuhr said in an article about the Republican victory in 1952, "American conservatism is not conservative at all in the traditional sense; it is a part of the traditional liberal movement, and it exhibits the defects of its creed, but it has not retained many of its virtues."

But neither is Niebuhr to be identified with a traditional conservatism. He may discover certain virtues therein, such as a better understanding of the role of power and interest, especially in international relations. He would join a conservative like Sir Winston Churchill in saying, of the social engineer's prediction that soon we shall be able to control even the thoughts in men's minds, that in that day he would be content to be dead. But a look at, say, Niebuhr's chapter on the ethics of the privileged classes in *Moral Man and Immoral Society,* or his critique of orthodoxy in *An Interpretation of Christian Ethics,* indicates that he is not really in sympathy with a conservatism even of the more domesticated sort. One suspects that if he were a Britisher, despite his appreciation of Sir Winston, he would be found in the Opposition. For conservatives' views, like everyone else's, are colored by their interest, and they overestimate the virtues and underestimate the injustices of the existing order and of their own position. They differ from their opponents not in their partiality but in their having more power to effectuate their views. They usually have inertia on their side too. What Niebuhr calls "relative justice" will usually not be with the conservatives, however cultured or humane or "new," but with their opponents.

The biggest irony is in relating Niebuhr to the conservatives' fond regard for religion as a help in the proper ordering of society. Russell Kirk, one of the writers working this new conservative vein, who finds conservatism to be a unified movement from the time of Edmund Burke right down to the present, sets forth as the very first principle of this conservative tradition a belief in the Providence of God. And there is a great deal of conservative talk about sin, especially original sin, and the need it is supposed to introduce for hierarchy and authority and prescription in society.

Niebuhr is not the father of all this but rather its most trenchant critic. Original sin is not, for him, just another name for "man's" being "evil," which then leads to some authoritarian politics; it is rather a part of the whole of Christian doctrine, from which it cannot very fruitfully be extracted. Original sin involves also an original righteousness; it is the result of a "fall," and a fall must be from some height. Man is not "evil," but of a unique and mixed nature that includes a "memory" of a righteousness which even his worst acts cannot wholly erase, and to which his uneasy conscience always attests. He has a capacity for justice that makes democracy possible, as well as a capacity for injustice that makes it necessary.

Niebuhr's position leads to a heightened, not a lowered, view of the true stature of man. It is man's actual performance, his failure to live in accord with his stature, of which Niebuhr takes a dim view. His appraisal of human nature is not just a negative one, which after all a lot of people do hold, but rather a problematic one.

Man lives in a tension between the law of love (which makes demands upon him relevant to every situation in life) and his constant failure to fulfill that law completely. If there are political consequences of his view, they are not conservative but quite the reverse: a constant criticism of the injustices that every social order in a fallen world contains, an unremitting effort to achieve the always greater but never final measure of justice that is possible. Niebuhr's doctrine of sin leads to a dynamic view of life; it leads neither to despair nor to complacency — those two supports of quietism and conservatism — but rather to a permanent reform.

Of course it is dangerous to draw specific political conclusions directly from religious doctrines; conservatives often fail to see this danger, which Niebuhr continually points out. He says that religion has often been a source of "confusion" in politics. The religious are always prone to an idolatry in which they confuse their own political programs with the will of the Almighty. They are tempted to think they can reason straight from some religious doctrine (like that of original sin) to a final political position. But no religious doctrine of itself solves any social problem. There is no substitute for concrete moral and political insight. Niebuhr wrote recently of the unwillingness of the European theologian Karl Barth wholeheartedly to condemn Communist tyranny: "The whole performance prompts revulsion against every pretension to derive detailed political judgments from ultimate theological positions. When a man lacks ordinary common sense in reacting against evil, no amount of theological sophistication will help him."

One cause of the ironic misinterpretation of Niebuhr is that he combines political wisdom, both practical and theoretical, with theological profundity; not many others do. He represents simultaneously diverse abilities and different currents of thought with such force and resolution that it is difficult for anyone else to hold together all the parts of what he says. Niebuhr's unique contribution depends upon these combinations of Christian doctrine and American pragmatic and democratic politics, of speculation and concrete wisdom, of thought and action. Thus it is hard to pass on the whole of what he says to anyone else. More is lost when Niebuhr himself is subtracted from Niebuhrianism than is usual in such cases, for such a large part of Niebuhrianism is what Niebuhr alone can do.

Because Niebuhr forcefully combines diverse talents he often is regarded with a gingerly and ambiguous mixture of awe, admiration, and mistrust. One encounters both in and out of the church counterparts of that good bishop in Detroit who, in introducing Niebuhr some years ago, was careful to disclaim all of Niebuhr's opinions before they were uttered, but assured his hearers that Niebuhr would "make them think."

Not all groups regard Niebuhr with any such mixture of attitudes; in some he is regarded with plain, old-fashioned, unambiguous dislike. He said once, during the prewar days when he was leading the interventionist fight against the deep-rooted isolationism in the Protestant church, "I wish some of these pacifists would hate Hitler more and me less." This dislike appears especially among some of the idealists who have felt the sting of Niebuhr's attack: pacifists, doctrinaire socialists, world-government people, do-gooders, and advocates of various one-shot solutions to world problems. Against them the Niebuhrian adjectives have rolled with telling effect: "sentimental," "idealist," "utopian," "irrelevant," "moralistic," "perfectionist." His reason for opposing such idealistic programs is grounded in his theology: They do not take account of the real nature of man and history; specifically, they ignore the facts of power and interest in society.

Niebuhr has always criticized the idealism of the liberals in American politics, but, it should be noted, as a friend who remained identified with their purposes. The testimony of liberals to what Niebuhr has meant to them makes this plain. A liberal lawyer: "To me, Reinhold Niebuhr is the intellectual and spiritual leader of the anti-Communist Left in the U.S." A liberal American historian and political writer: "Niebuhr showed that it was possible to fight hard for social betterment and reform without surrendering to sentimentality." The editor of a liberal New York daily paper: "To me the real impact of his position is to deepen our awareness of human frailty without destroying our belief in the capacity of man to combat social injustice." A founder of A.D.A.: "More than anyone else he has forced the liberal-radical movement into realistic and pragmatic terms." A recent candidate for President: "I think there are few contemporaries whose literacy and vitality I envy more, whose breadth, perception, and social morality I admire more. Has he had any effect on me? I don't know, but I hope so."

Not all liberals have any such hope. Many hold ironic misinterpretations of Niebuhr like those of the conservatives. Since in Niebuhr's books liberals always have "illusions," we might set down some liberal illusions about Niebuhr.

The first is that he is a "pessimist," "gloomy," and "defeatist," representing the dour outlook of effete "continentals" against American optimism and activism. Actually, nobody could be less melancholic, less morbid and defeatist than

Niebuhr. He criticizes, in a very American way, the irrelevance of much of the contemplative and mystical stand in religion. It is his vigor, his constant, confident, practical action, which many of his admirers — his very American admirers — find most impressive. As John Gunther once said, to interview him is like throwing paper airplanes into an electric fan. His books deal almost exclusively with the doctrines — chiefly of man and of history — that are most immediately relevant to the practical tasks of life. As to his alleged gloom and pessimism, genuine optimism can afford to be hard-headed about the immediate situation without despair because of an ultimate confidence. And that's Niebuhr.

Another illusion of some liberals is that Niebuhr is an irrational dogmatist. Anthony West, in a strange review in the *New Yorker* in which he referred to Niebuhr as a "liberal" theologian, argued, as nearly as I can make out, like this: Niebuhr is against reason; reason is the basis of the United Nations; the United Nations is the best hope for peace and mankind; therefore Niebuhr is against peace and mankind. The logical form of this may be satisfactory but the proposition on which it is built is mistaken. One feels about this business of being "against reason" that the thing to do with reason is not to defend it but to use it, and Niebuhr does that. He does it in a thoroughgoing way that admits the unreasonable elements that are present in life, especially social life. Which is more rational, to deny these on the basis of some abstract belief in reason or to free the intelligence of illusions and to admit what is really there?

Niebuhr's reasoning is not deductive and systematic but empirical and pragmatic — once again in the American style. He is always testing theoretical constructions against experience. He is primarily a critical thinker, rushing on to indicate a truth, not stopping to formalize it. Therefore his style may leave something to be desired. He is never a definitional writer, carefully polishing his terms and relating them to one another in a system; rather he points to truth that can be observed, sometimes using sweeping generalizations to point to it. The phrases he uses constantly — "too simple," "too confident," "which does not recognize," "does not do justice to," "does not take account of" — are all inexact. He does not say what would be just simple enough, or confident enough, or just when precise justice had been done to the element with which he is concerned. Rather, he makes his judgment and leaves his reader to confirm it from his own experience. The ability to follow Niebuhr therefore depends in part on making the same kind of observation of life that he makes. He is quite the opposite of a dogmatist, arbitrarily applying some *a priori* scheme to the facts. He is an upsetter of dogma, challenging the complacent acceptance of uncriticized assumptions. This is not always noted because the secular and "liberal" traditions he challenges may not be conscious of their own dogmas.

A third illusion is that he is an anachronism, preaching something long since out of date. Some moderns perhaps would make such a charge against any serious Christian position. If one avoids that dogma, then a case might be made for the rather special relevance of Niebuhr's Christianity to our time. He sees a central truth with which our age is concerned, the relativity of all positions; he speaks for a central virtue which our time has recognized, self-criticism. Niebuhr is most radically aware of the partiality of all perspectives and the relativity of all cultures; he and his followers resist the "absolutizing" of any "relative." In a way what Niebuhr does is to take our twentieth-century understanding of cultural relativism and apply it more thoroughly than its secular spokesmen. He takes the awareness of the need for self-criticism and self-correction, which comes partly from a modern scientific outlook, and applies it even to *that* outlook. But Niebuhr sees the relativity of all points of view, including his own, without falling into a final relativism which denies that there is truth. He does this by standing within the Christian church, which has, and yet does not have, the truth. The church which, as Niebuhr says, has survived like Noah's Ark despite the storm without and the smell within, points to a truth beyond its own stating of it. Before God, who is absolute, the religious man knows all human positions to be relative.

Sometimes some of Niebuhr's admirers seem to assume that his social thought can be detached from the Christian faith from which it has been derived. Sometimes, too, intellectual admirers of Niebuhr seem to look upon him as an entirely unique phenomenon, unparalleled, arising apparently without relation to the American Protestantism in which he was born, in which he grew up and was educated, and in which he has spent his whole life and career preaching and teaching. Against all this I venture a suggestion possibly reflecting the special interest of my own partial position: Niebuhr's insight depends upon the faith and the community of faith of which he is a part. He is a product of American Protestant Christianity.

And here, if you can stand it, is just one more irony. For in producing Niebuhr, American Protestantism did better than it intended. But then, that's what it always does. Dwight L. Moody converts young college men at revivals; they become leaders of a liberal Protestantism that repudiates Moody's fundamentalism and revivalism; Bishop McConnell and Walter Rauschenbusch inspire young men with the vision of Christian social idealism; the young men turn out to be Niebuhrs who expose the deficiencies of Christian social idealism.

And what then happens with the followers of Niebuhr? It is to be hoped that we in turn will make another restatement, for a new age, of an eternal message. Perhaps you have noticed in some of us who are products of his teaching a certain derivative quality, a rather wooden way of repeating what we have been taught about "sin" and so on. That won't do. A great European Christian noted the difference between Faust's saying, at the end of a life spent pursuing knowledge, "I now see that we can nothing know," and a freshman saying the same thing his first day in college. A young preacher in Detroit, asked by a parishioner why he didn't preach more on the blood atonement, said he thought he ought to wait until he had shed some himself. There may be a problem with some of us followers of that young preacher, now become this eminent theologian, that we just repeat what he has said without recapturing its meaning in the context of our lives.

But the statements of a living faith, unlike rational propositions, do depend upon the context in which they are spoken, and the life and community out of which they are spoken. Protestantism, which is a living faith, is therefore always in need of restatement in new historical situations; it is always rejecting its founders, or rather, affirming them by partly rejecting them. It is at its best a prophetic movement, and the way to follow prophets is not to repeat what they said in past ages but to recapture what they meant, now in relation to a new present age.

So Protestantism is always surprising itself, turning up prophets whom the main body of the church didn't intend or want to turn up. In our time the chief of these is Reinhold Niebuhr.

Part V

The "Moral Force"
behind Dulles' Diplomacy

August 9, 1956

A LIFE editorial once asked, "Should U.S. Policy Be Moral?"
The answer turned out to be Yes. How was U.S. policy to be
made moral? By supporting John Foster Dulles. ". . . his
policies have a religious motivation . . . he is trying to put
U.S. policy back on an explicitly moral basis . . ."

But putting the U.S. policy *back* on a moral basis, after its
years presumably in some amoral Democratic limbo, has
proved to be a little more difficult than at first it seemed. Take
the recent administration brouhaha over "neutralism." When
Dulles spoke at Iowa State College on June 9 he seemed to
contradict the genial words the President had spoken, at a
press conference three days earlier, and to lay down a strict
moral line about neutrality. At least, Mr. Luce's *Time* Magazine, always alert to Moral Issues, seemed to think so. It was
not an ordinary case, for *Time's* man Dulles was in the unusual
position of trying to cover someone else's blooper. It was not
an easy case, for *Time* had to choose between two kindred
spirits, both usually on the moral side: Eisenhower and Dulles.
But the Luce publications do not hesitate where Absolute
right and wrong is at stake: Ike had strayed.

In the gentle words he spoke for neutralism, said *Time*, Ike
"got in over his head." In his claim that the U.S. itself had

long been a neutral, he made a "disconcerting mis-statement of U.S. history." His whole effort to treat the subject resulted in "a blurred statement of U.S. foreign policy." Dulles then appeared in *Time's* pages as a sounder, deeper, stronger figure, an ethical lecturer, "correcting the slip" of a blundering President: "at week's end, Secretary of State Dulles tried to repair the damage." *Time* had Dulles straighten out Ike's views on U.S. history, and put at the heart of its story of this little breakthrough on the moral front, with apparent approval, the paragraph from Dulles' speech that linked neutralism — or perhaps "the principle of neutrality," or something — with the word "immoral."

But then after Richard Nixon, another prominent moralist, had twice entered the discussion (once on each side); and after considerable boiling around among foreign diplomats about U.S. views on neutralism; and after Dulles, under questioning at a press conference, had not explained his views but claimed that there was no conflict between them and the President's; and after Prime Minister Nehru had kidded the U.S. for its apparently contradictory views and chided Dulles and Nixon for wanting everybody to think as they did, there came at last on July 11 a further amplification from Dulles about the immorality of neutralism. It was an explanation that just about explained it away.

Mr. Dulles recalled the complicated language of his original statement, which left open as one possible meaning just that "being unconcerned for the fate of other nations" was immoral. Membership in the UN, said Dulles, shows concern for other nations. Even for countries, like Switzerland, that have not joined the UN, there was an escape clause about "exceptional circumstances" in his Iowa State speech. The Secretary admitted that there were "very few, if any" countries that actually fitted his definition of immoral neutrality. Having, in the *New York Times'* words, "vexed" some and "puzzled" all of Washington's diplomatic corps, having stirred the free-flowing moral juices of *Time,* Inc., having given Nehru a chance to lead the Commonwealth prime ministers in a laugh and a growl at the U.S., the "moral" statement was at last retired to the harmless shelf of abstract principle, inapplicable to any discernible nation. One wonders if it should have been taken down from there in the first place.

Dulles, the world's most eminent spokesman for Moral Force in World Affairs, is a more complicated man than most of those with whom he is associated. For the President, the Vice-President, or the Secretary of Defense, for example, there is a standard set of adjectives, an expected position, a relatively clear political personality. But not for Mr. Dulles. He is a complex man in the middle of a simple administration.

His story is not that of his party colleagues, Vandenberg and Wiley, nationalists converted by events to internationalism; nor is it that of his religious associates, Christian idealists brought by new currents of thought to realism; nor is it that of fellow experts on world affairs, drawn from trust in International Law to a greater awareness of power. Rather, all these different elements seem to be simultaneously present in him, now one and now another subordinated. One is never quite sure which side of him is going to be up.

On reading his speeches one is struck by the quality of many of them. His thought is clearer and more sophisticated, his language more varied and precise, than that of most of his colleagues — certainly than that of his chief. But President Eisenhower manages, despite his trouble with language, to make his larger meaning come through; Mr. Dulles manages, despite his greater facility with language, to keep his larger meaning obscure. With Ike the words are fuzzy but the real intention clear; with Dulles the words are clear, but the real intention fuzzy.

This complicatedness may be the result of a curious kind of overdevelopment. The most familiar part of this is his hyperpreparation in diplomacy. With his grandfather and uncle, who were both Secretaries of State, and with those long years of yearning and studying to follow them, he may be overtrained for the post. He does not need to rely on the staff work of a modern foreign office. He knows the job too well to learn it.

A former foreign service officer says the trouble is he started in too high a place. As a college boy he was taken by his uncle, the Secretary of State under Wilson, to the 1907 Hague Peace Conference, and has lived among the virtuosos of high level negotiation ever since. He entered diplomacy at the top, and never had to learn its arts of listening and keeping quiet, or reporting and coordinating, from the bottom.

His picture of a Secretary seems to be drawn from a romantic version of the past, when the personal diplomat appeared as an individual performer on the international stage. Leaving the State Department to mind its own business, whatever that might be, Dulles flies to London, Paris, Manila, Denver, Duck Island, New Delhi, Cairo, and Geneva, as his own ambassador and his own negotiator. Nonvisitation becomes a diplomatic weapon, as when, after EDC was beaten, in 1954, he pointedly did not stop to see Mendès-France. Personal visitation becomes a normal channel of policy. The Secretary appears not as the chief of a department or the administrator in a government or the leader of a country's policy but rather an individual confidently performing his individual role. "It is silly," he said on television, "to go at it the old-fashioned way of exchanging notes, which take a month perhaps before you get a good understanding" when "by overnight flight" and "talking a few minutes face-to-face" the good understanding can be reached at once. But, as Walter Lippmann said, "Mr. Dulles has traveled 310,000 miles, and can it be said that the globe is studded with good understandings?"

Mr. Dulles also has the overarticulateness and assurance of the lawyer, skilled in advocacy and the fine points of the law, able to develop all the elements of each side of the case, to make multiple and varying readings, and to remember the small print when it is necessary. His words — on neutralism, liberation, positive loyalty, massive retaliation, brinks of wars — seem often to be surrounded by a haze of qualifications and provisos, of interpretations, misinterpretations, and reinterpretations. Also, he seems well supplied with the lawyer's trust in formulas and pacts, in written words and formal agreements.

There is one more overdevelopment — as a partisan. Having been a prominent representative of bipartisan foreign policy, he seems eager to take the curse off that by heaping blame on the "Democrat" Party and paying strictest attention to Republican needs.

But behind these well-known aspects of Dulles, as the overtrained diplomat, the oversubtle lawyer, the over-Republican campaigner, may be a still more important aspect, the one that Mr. Luce's publications unwittingly portray: the overconfident moralist. This may be the core of it, both the cause and the explanation of his lack of restraint in the other roles. "Into the counsels of his workaday diplomacy," the Luce people have explained, "he is admitting a criterion of Absolute right and wrong."

*

Fifty-odd years ago John Foster Dulles was attending four services every Sunday in the First Presbyterian Church of Watertown, New York, of which his father was the minister. In addition, every Sunday he would memorize ten verses of a hymn. As the Secretary has recalled, though it was a holy day, it was not exactly a day of rest.

Almost twenty years ago John Foster Dulles attended two international conferences: one, a League-sponsored gathering in Geneva, on a subject in which he has long been interested, "Peaceful Change"; the other, a religious meeting in Oxford, on church and state. The contrast between the "power politics" of the first and the idealism of the second made an impression on him. After what he has called "thirty years of futility" in dealing with the evildoings of nations, he saw that "there is no way to solve the great perplexing international problems except by bringing to bear on them the force of Christianity."

Fifteen years ago Mr. Dulles became the chairman and chief mover of the Protestant churches' Commission to study the Bases of a Just and Durable Peace. "He more than any other person," wrote one of his colleagues in that venture, "was responsible for shaping the mind of the Protestant churches respecting the post-war world."

Dulles became one of those almost professional laymen who are taken up into the upper reaches of the churches' bureaucracies, a region teeming with conferences, and flowing with the ink of resolutions. Mr. Dulles added mightily to the flow. As American Protestantism's chief committee-sitter on international affairs, his reputation in the churches became immense.

When in 1953 Dulles became Secretary of State there was considerable gratification among many Protestants that their man had made it. A cartoon in the *Christian Herald* showed this feeling: Dulles appeared as a cook, about to mix a bowl of foreign policy; he was reaching for canisters labeled "moral leadership," "religious background," "Christian ethics," and "churchmanship." The caption proudly claimed: "He brought some fine ingredients along."

But after eating this cooking for three years, many of his admirers find it has a bitter taste they didn't expect.

This is partly the result of their impossibly idealistic expectations of what a certified good man could do. But it is partly also the result of being too unequivocally certified to that status.

Just as Mr. Dulles' unique training in diplomacy means he can carry on without consulting his staff, so his unique position in "moral leadership" means he can speak with authority in that field. Maybe it would be better in both fields not to be so well qualified — and therefore to have to depend more on the give and take with others.

In a commencement speech he gave back in 1946 Mr. Dulles said, "We laugh about the puritanism and austerity of the past. But that is the way our forebears trained their moral muscles for the struggle for freedom. Today these muscles are flabby." One sometimes has the impression that Mr. Dulles, far from being flabby, with those years of exercise in the specialized gymnasium of professional moral leadership, had himself become morally muscle-bound.

This overdeveloped ethical confidence may help even to account for the other, dominant element of his public personality, his toughness. The Presbyterian Elder, when he ran for the Senate in 1949, turned out to be a surprisingly rough campaigner. This spokesman for moral force, when he became Secretary, showed a startling ability to accommodate to the

hard requirements of Republican politics in the era of Mc-
Carthy. This expert on International Justice and Goodwill
became the stiffest talker on the team, not only toward the
Communists, but also toward neutrals and allies. This spokesman for the Just and Durable Peace became the advocate of
"massive retaliatory power."

There is even that odd touch of swashbuckling, or of der-
ring-do, that keeps cropping up in Dulles. The "Dulles Gam-
bled and Won" article in *Life*, with its gratified reminiscence
of his virtuosity on the brink, is a notable example. But even
back in 1950 Dulles was thinking about foreign policy this way:

"The stakes are the greatest for which men have ever
played. I recall, as a boy, reading Robert Louis Stevenson's
story 'The Suicide Club.' The club members were dealt cards
every Saturday night and the one who drew the ace of clubs
had to kill within twenty-four hours the one who drew the
ace of spades. I read and re-read that story with bated breath.
Today we are all, in a sense, members of a suicide club with
the difference for us it is not just a game of luck: we have the
opportunity to prevent the suicide of humanity."

All of this may reflect that compensatory worldliness that is
often adopted by those who are formally connected with goodness. The preacher says a cuss word or tells a joke, to make
it plain he is a real guy after all. A man who has known
Dulles over the years says he overdoes the aspect of the
rugged realist just because he is eager to avoid any accusation
of sentimentality his churchly doings might bring forth.

But the Calvinist-Puritan-Presbyterian tradition Dulles
comes from is not as sentimental as some strands of American
Protestantism, anyway. In that Watertown Presbyterian
Church when Dulles went there, there would not have been
as much talk of love and harmony and brotherhood as one
would get later, farther west, and in more liberal churches.

There would probably be more talk of Law and Righteousness and the solid, sober Calvinistic virtues.

Mr. Dulles represents characteristic virtues of that tradition: an unfrivolous sense of responsibility, an untiring pursuit of duty, an unbending opposition to what he regards as evil. He may also represent characteristic vices, including an undue confidence that one has identified evil for sure, and that it is on the other fellow's side. When you have it arranged that way, you can talk tough and be moral at the same time.

Mr. Dulles, whose political understanding is better than that of many of his religious supporters, tried in his years with Protestant agencies to bring their airborne hopes down nearer to the ground of possibility. He spoke regularly of the "discipline of the achievable." But though his politics was more sophisticated than those of many Protestant colleagues, his philosophy was not.

"Moral force is the only force that can accomplish great things in the world," he would say.

"The great issue of our time is the acceptance by individual human beings of the dictates of the moral law," he would say.

Such affirmations may serve just as self-endorsement for those who hear them. Hearers tend to think of themselves as the prime bearer of that moral force and acceptors of that moral law. Without some more critical philosophy, the simple moral ideas may be separated from actions; as in Mr. Dulles' case, they may provide very little indication of what a believer will actually do. What they may provide, instead, is a self-righteousness in the doing of it.

Alongside his complicated daily political operation was a simple ethical outlook; what is lacking, in between, displaced by the moralism, is a political philosophy adequate for the time and position in which Dulles serves.

Or maybe what's missing is intuitive understanding and

empathy. For the President, that serves in place of a philosophy. Most points-of-view in the middle of the twentieth
century, including religious ones, have some way to understand diversities of points-of-view and differences of cultures.
But the exercise of those Puritan muscles on Absolute right
and wrong can leave a man unable to bend, to see how right
and wrong may look from the very different position of, say,
a Nehru. Without some sense of the relativity of cultures,
the American moralist can end up talking a language almost
no one else in the world can understand.

What is worse, the language may not mean a thing. There
is a habit among those for whom preaching is a central activity to delight just in the sound of the stern, demanding
words and then, like Channing's father, to go whistling home
to a warm house and a big dinner, anyway. Sometimes one
feels in Henry Luce's paragraphs about Dulles that what he
wants is just for somebody to *say* and to keep saying, that we
are good and the Communists are not.

But the language does mean something: it means at least
that the speaker wants something he can support with *fervor*.
The man of this background often is unhappy with the cool
and rational practitioners of the diplomatic art, because there
is nothing in their counsel, about restraint, limited wars, and
the modest pursuit of the national interest, that one can respond to with *zeal*. The issues of the world politics, of whether
humanity will draw the wrong card in that suicide game,
are dramatic and moving; they should be dealt with in a way
that a man can respond to with a revival enthusiasm.

Mr. Dulles can do it. To the National Council of Presby-
terian Men, for example, he told the story of the Japanese
Peace Treaty, of which he himself had been chief artisan:
"Four years ago, speaking here, I said that moral power was

the greatest power in the world . . . Now here is a new exhibit: the Japanese Peace Treaty.

"There were two possible powers to invoke, the power of evil or the power of good . . . We had to go all out in one direction or another. Half measures would not avail . . ." Mr. Dulles explained which of the two powers he had invoked, all the way. That is the kind of foreign policy that the evangelistic heritage really can respond to. Of course, others gave a slightly different picture of the Japanese Treaty, particularly Mr. Dulles' own pressure — despite a promise to the British — to make Japan recognize Nationalist China. But details like that would have spoiled the dramatic simplicity.

The emphasis on zeal, boldness, and dynamism recurs continually in Dulles, and usually in conjunction with morality. A related note is his putting the best face on everything, finding diplomatic gains for us even in the Geneva Foreign Ministers' Conference, avoiding any admission of weakness or loss, claiming that our system of alliances is better than ever, asserting that changes in Russia since Stalin's death are the result of our own dynamic policies.

The "liberation" theme, set over against the "negative, sterile" doctrine of "containment" is an example. Mr. Dulles, its chief proponent, said that since it would be immoral and undynamic to leave the satellites under Soviet control, the United States should proclaim its intention to "liberate" them. This energetic declaration of intent, however, was all that could be done; on taking office, with a few lame and unconcluded gestures against the Yalta Conference, the dynamic Eisenhower-Dulles policy more or less forgot about "liberation." When Poles revolted in Poznan, the silence from Duck Island was impressive. Liberation turned out to be not as worthy as a policy as it had sounded as a campaign theme. For one thing, it gave our European allies a real fright; for another, it seemed to encourage friends behind the Iron Curtain to rise, and to destroy themselves, when we had no real intention to go to war to rescue them. The favorable response of Polish voters in Hamtramck and Buffalo to the "liberation" theme gave to its no doubt sincere proponents a mixture of motives; it is always helpful when ethical convictions turn out handily to serve one's more earthbound interests. But in the end these splendid sounds may prove to be neither dynamic nor even particularly moral, after all.

Perhaps American foreign policy should try to *be* moral, and not keep labeling itself as such. Perhaps it should try rather to present programs that evoke zeal, than to drum up that quality by talking about it. The words may mean nothing; they may rouse passions where thought would serve better. Worse, they may forge an unassailable ratification of one group's preferences. The diplomatic moralizer has a weapon others do not have: he can simply draw a line that excludes some policies as immoral. Maybe the policies that Mr. Dulles does not like can be proved mistaken, but it ought to be necessary to *prove* it, and not just to assert it from the unassailable pinnacle of Absolute right and wrong.

Time Magazine showed how this may work in one exposition of Dulles' policies: "He believes that where a nation holds a trusteeship against an organized evil, as the U.S. does, successful, realistic policy takes on a positive moral value." We may seem to say that, by a convenient arrangement of history, because our enemy now is evil, whatever we do successfully to oppose him is good.

It may be Mr. Dulles' self-confidence, as the man who is right, the moral tough guy, that explains his remarkable collection of gaffes. He told State Department employees that he would expect "positive loyalty," thereby adding to their problem of morale. He told European governments that unless EDC was enacted, it would be hard to get Congress to continue foreign aid, thereby seeming to use U.S. money as a weapon against its allies. He said the defeat of Adenauer by the German voters would be "disastrous," thereby adding to the impression that the U.S. bluntly interferes in other countries' internal politics. He suggested that the U.S. pro-Italian Trieste policy might be revised, thereby angering Italy without appreciably pleasing Yugoslavia. He called off aid to Israel, and then, after a visit from the Republican candidate for Mayor of New York City, had the department reinstate it, thereby seeming to tie U.S. policy most obviously to the needs of local politics. He joined in calling Goa a "province," thereby seeming to take the Portuguese and colonial side, angering the Indians. When he gave General Neguib a pistol of President Eisenhower's, as a gift, he said, "This is for keeping the peace, not for war." When he was given a Hebrew Bible by Ben-Gurion, he asked whether it included the New Testament. On another occasion he said that Arabs dislike Jews because Mohammed was killed by a Jew. In Karachi, he spoke of the need for building up local forces to resist aggression, which annoyed India; in New Delhi, he guaranteed that India would find the U.S. on her side if Pakistan attacked, which annoyed Pakistan. It may be that because he thinks of himself as sort of a moral "poor man's Metternich," he seems also to be "the man born with a silver foot in his mouth."

Ideals have a way of slipping downward, beginning as means of self-examination, ending as means of self-aggrandizement. "Freedom" can be the battle cry of those who free slaves, or the slogan of those who increase profits; "moral law" can be for trying ourselves, or for exposing the deficiencies of those who stand in the way; "individual dignity" can be the source of respect for an employee, or the excuse for breaking his union. The invocation of the spiritual difference between us and the Communists may serve to clarify and criticize our actions, or only to justify what we are already doing on other grounds. These moral lawyers have to be watched, particularly when their high claims really serve a feeling of complacency.

The continual insistence that we have the "moral initiative," as though the proclaiming of it made it so, may have this worse result: by its tone and language it may offend those with whom it is important to have that initiative (say in Southeast Asia or in the Arab states) and thereby prevent its own claims from being realized. We unite freedom, morality and commitment to the U.S. in a bundle; the uncommitted nations don't see it that way. These ethical claims can be the source of cocky lack of restraint even toward allies. There seems to be the feeling that because we are right, we can act unilaterally; proclaim a righteous policy of "united action" in Indo-China, for example, without consulting France and England.

Mr. Dulles said on coming into office that his would be a policy of "openness, simplicity, and righteousness"; the "righteousness" may be a cause of the increased isolation of the United States from neutrals and allies that some see as the great danger of the present day.

Leaves from the Notebook
of a Tamed Idealist

1. THE PEOPLE AND FOREIGN POLICY

1957

The relationship of most of us to "foreign policy" is like Stephen Leacock's relationship to the banking business — as a depositor. Few of us who speak about the subject have the knowledge of the man who does the work — but we do have connections with the effects.

The opinion of the public is an important consideration in the making of foreign policy; but foreign policy is a peculiarly difficult field for the public to have useful opinions about. A combination of these two points makes for headaches. Once, perhaps, international relations consisted simply of diplomats negotiating with each other within a carefully established set of rules. But now (often to the dismay of the diplomats) the public crowds into the picture. The inclusive nature of modern society, of modern war and of modern movements like Communism, makes this crowding inevitable.

Wars may once have been far-off events which states fought with each other using armies of professional soldiers. Today wars are total; they gather in every citizen and all parts of life. We are now engaged in a world conflict in which all sorts of nonmilitary and nondiplomatic considerations come into play, and the opinion of great publics around the world is a consideration for any statesman.

And the foreign policy of a democracy cannot be kept out of political campaigns. In the United States we hear much about bipartisanship in foreign affairs, especially from the party in power, and there has been a significant core of agreement on foreign policy between the two major parties in the country. But this agreement can be supported by both parties in Washington only so long as no part of it becomes galling to a significant part of the American people.

The attitudes of the parties toward the Korean war are an example of this. Although Mr. Truman's original decision in Korea met with wide bipartisan favor, it later became a cause of bitter partisan division.

In the spring of 1953 the presidential assistant, Mr. Gabriel Hauge, stated that during the 1952 campaign the American people forced Mr. Eisenhower to talk about the Korean war. Everywhere the Eisenhower train went during that campaign, he said, local Republicans insisted that the main issue — even the only issue — was Korea. That one got a response; that one people were feeling.

The difficulties of American public opinion dealing with foreign policy come from its being held by a public, and by one that is American. The difficulty of its being public is pointed up in a statement from a recent book on communications: "Since common experience is essential to communications, the greater the number to be reached, the simpler the communication must be." But by their very nature problems in foreign policy are complex.

The difficulty of its being American involves our long national tradition of isolation, of concentration on our domestic problems. Moreover, foreign policy problems require an art at which we Americans are not particularly adept, namely, the inexact calculations of power, the manipulation of subtle interests.

Our genius is for the external and the functional; our difficulty is in dealing with imponderables — with questions of value. We are used to weighing and measuring. We want to know where we are going and when we are going to get there and when we can expect to return. But these are the very things that we cannot know if we enter the uncertain world of foreign affairs, a world where all is inexact and exhausting, where American "know-how" will often be frustrated in its search for the ready answer.

2. TWO REALLY REALISTIC REALISTS

1958

George Kennan and Dean Acheson now disagree with each other about "disengagement" in Europe, and also, in that connection at least, about the nature of power (Mr. Acheson finds Mr. Kennan's view "mystical," while Mr. Kennan finds Mr. Acheson's "overmilitarized"). But despite their present disagreement, they have both been part of one large movement of thought, that in the last decade has changed American thinking about the subject of power, and about world affairs. They have been the two most eminent representatives, among practitioners, of "realism" — that is, of the dilemmas-hazards-limitations-paradoxes-ambiguities-responsibilities-and-perils kind of hardheaded but not cynical reflection of politics. Most of us who have come of age politically since the Second World War have come to accept something of this outlook. I think, however, that we ought to be selective and critical in doing so.

The "realistic" attack upon what Mr. Kennan called, in some famous paragraphs, the "legalistic-moralistic" stand in American attitudes toward international politics is almost as familiar, by now, as the phenomenon against which it is directed.* So is the parallel attack on "utopianism" and "idealism." Perhaps, indeed, almost too familiar. Our "realism" is not, or should not be, the whole of a political outlook; it is simply one necessary part of it. But the political realism that has developed in the United States may sometimes be overly emphatic, because it is overreacting to the American atmosphere.

I think the effect of our "realism" has been on the whole beneficial: we have been learning or teaching a first lesson in politics that we Americans need. But a first lesson is not an entire position, and especially not when it is chiefly a polemical reaction against a broad public attitude.

The "realists," perhaps I should explain, include the most distinguished political thinkers of our time: in addition to Mr. Kennan and Mr. Acheson, this group would include most all of Hans Morgenthau, but especially his earlier things; one half of Reinhold Niebuhr (he is also an effective critic of others of the realists); one side of Walter Lippmann, at least in an earlier phase; E. H. Carr, as a British representative; and many other influential diplomatists and teachers of international relations, together with some theologians, political philosophers, and journalists. This has been the chief strand of theory about foreign relations, in this country, since the Second World War — a strand that has effectively overthrown the Wilsonian idealism of the interwar period; that has recovered virtues from an older European tradition of "reason of state," and an American tradition from Admiral Mahan and Theodore Roosevelt,

* George Kennan, *American Diplomacy, 1900–1950* (Chicago: University of Chicago Press, 1951), pages 95–101.

although it is different from these; and that has improved American understandings of "power" and of "national interest" and of the "art of the possible." It may be too much to speak of a "school" of Realism, as is sometimes done, since these men differ from each other markedly, and since the themes they hold in common do not constitute a theory but only a "disposition." The "Idealism" that is set over against "Realism" (mostly by the Realists themselves), moreover, is not ordinarily a serious structured political position — a real opponent — but rather just a naïve outlook on the part of a public. Nevertheless, the realist themes have seemed to many of us to have been of the first rank of importance.

However, sometimes these themes have too much shown their polemical origin, reflecting the overreaction of which I have spoken.

An example of this would be the attitude toward the "people." The Wilsonians drew a sharp line between rulers (mostly bad) who caused wars and troubles, and the people (wise, virtuous and peace-loving) who could be appealed to over rulers' heads, and counted on to support what is right. Some realists draw something of the same line — between leaders of experts or diplomats on the one hand, and "public opinion" on the other; they evaluate their respective merit, however, in the opposite way. Prevailing public opinion, said Walter Lippmann, has been destructively wrong at the critical junctures in the United States foreign policy. Many of our unwise policies, says George Kennan, result from executive acquiescence in short-term trends in public opinion. Often the policy-makers, says Hans Morgenthau, "must either sacrifice good policy upon the altar of public opinion, or by devious means gain popular support for policies whose true nature they conceal . . ." What emerges is a negative picture of "the pub-

lic," a positive picture of the expert, or diplomat, and a sharp
separation of the two. "Diplomacy" and the diplomat appear
as the "answer" in much realist writing.

Of course, it is hard to be clear about "the public" and "the
expert," but surely stereotypes or sentimentality about either
are to be resisted, and wholehearted rejection is not a better
attitude toward "the people" than wholehearted endorsement.
In realists one sometimes discerns a notion of the expert or the
diplomat above politics, a man pure and undefiled by the errors
of the public, and unstained by the political process. The figures of speech that George Kennan once allowed himself to
use, for example (in a speech to the American Historical Association), are revealing: the diplomat appears as the doctor
working on peculiarly unpleasant diseases, or as the mechanic
working on a badly designed car; he appears, that is, as the
technician, himself not responsible for, or a part of, the problem, who brings his expertise, from outside as it were, to bear
upon this difficult and distasteful task. But surely the diplomat
and the expert student are part of the process, related to it
and to its problems; they do have a connection with that
"public."

And high professional involvement is not without its own
limitations. Wisdom and justice require, it seems to me, a tension between the "realistic" things the expert and the man-in-
power know (about the limits and the difficulties) and the
vision that challenges these, that the nonexpert out-of-power
may be more free to entertain. I sometimes felt, when I was
teaching the "realism" that I had been taught, that I was
simply passing on the ideology of the professionals.

Sometimes this ideology of professionals (it is more than
that, really, I know) seems also to share the fault of its idealistic opponent in quite another way: being extreme and insistent

about an abstract formula. This "realism" appears with two faces: the careful, discriminating, empirical face, insisting that we have to start with the particular situation and its concrete limitations (this face I accept completely myself) and another face, full of abstractions and generalizations about Power and Interest and how nations always behave. This seems to me more dubious. It is joined, sometimes, with something else borrowed from the idealist: a perfectionistic attitude.

The idealist comes to the everyday political world with gigantic expectations: peace, total disarmament, world law, world government, universal justice. He is therefore inclined to be impatient with every actually practicing statesman, and with both political parties, and with most of the past political history of the nation, if not indeed of the human race, and with all presently available political possibilities, because all of these fall short of his great expectations. Surprisingly, the realistic bent, when it becomes a fierce and insistent position, may be the same — perfectionistic realism, as it were. Almost no one, with the possible exception of the founding fathers, has come up to some realists' high standards for international political behavior; so it is, perhaps, in Mr. Kennan's *American Diplomacy,* and so it is certainly in Mr. Morgenthau's book called *In Defense of the National Interest.*

This book of Mr. Morgenthau's also shows the capitalized and underlined overinsistence upon particular formulas that sometimes may be found on this wing. If the utopian and moralizer had oversimple formulas about "collective security" and "aggression" and "world law," so we realists may have the same about "power" and about the "national interest." After fiercely denouncing utopianisms and idealisms, failures of will and failures of leadership, right down through American history, Mr. Morgenthau rises at the end of his book to passionate italics and reverent capitals, in what appears to be a kind of litany of praise for the *"one guiding star, one thought, one rule for action:* THE NATIONAL INTEREST!"

A wise domestic political hand made an illuminating remark about this group in international affairs: these anti-moralists in foreign policy, he said can be *very* moralistic about domestic politics — quite unrealistic about the kinds of pressures actual, live, and fallible politicians do have to face. (One is reminded of Mr. Kennan's very negative remarks about Congress.) The realism may begin, so to speak, at the water's edge.

The more important "peril" (if I may use a well-worn realist word), however, is not that we react to the opposite pole from utopians and moralizers, but rather that, while trying to answer them, we too much take over their definition of the problem. We may simply take the morals-and-politics question as posed by them, and give a different answer to it. Instead we should change the question. We should change the terms fundamentally. The whole idealist-realist business has become rather sterile, I think, because we have not done so. I can illustrate and explain what I mean by reference again to Mr. Acheson and Mr. Kennan.

Mr. Acheson once wrote, criticizing moralizers about world politics, that "one cannot find in ethics or aesthetics alone a complement of tools for dealing with relations between states." * He said that into these relations there "enter factors governed by forces that operate in the physical rather than the metaphysical world." He added that "there also enters human conduct, which all too often is neither moral nor ethical nor controllable by exhortation." He said elsewhere that

---

* The quotations from Mr. Acheson come from an address, "Morality, Moralism, and Diplomacy," given at the University of Florida in Gainsville, February 20, 1958, and later published in *The Yale Review*.

"morality is a branch of idealism, which affirms the pre-eminence of the product of mind and spirit in determining reality." Now, all this seems to me a confusion. A serious reference to standards of value of course need not be tied to any such idealistic view — to any notion that human conduct is "controllable by exhortation," or that the physical "factors" can be ignored, or that "mind and spirit" "determines" reality. What Mr. Acheson has done here is to take over his opponent's conception: that all ethical judgment is inseparable from utopian expectations.

A popular idealism characteristically has expected huge and beneficent results from simple, evangelical appeals to the enthusiastic decision of the will: from a change of heart, from a great crusade. It sees optimism and voluntarism as necessary to moral responsibility: unless one believe that universal moral ideals can be realized in fact, by our own effort, and soon, then, it is implied, we will all lapse into cynicism, despair, and immorality. It is felt that to defend freedom as a goal, one must insist that there is a huge area of freedom as a fact; it is felt that to defend the "worth" and "dignity" of the individual, one must also insist upon the mammoth importance of individuals' actions in society and man's action in history. Any hint of determinism or even social conditioning is resisted as a threat to moral responsibility. Characteristically the holders of this view resist any suggestion of the relativity of moral notions, since they feel they must hold to those "absolutes" in order to hold to anything as good or right. Therefore they blind themselves to most of the political facts — to the existence ideologies, the pervasiveness of power, and the depth of collective experience — because they feel that to see these things would be to lose all moral conviction.

But when the observant political man noticed that there was

more to the world than was dreamt of in the idealist's philosophy, he also tended to assume that explicit ethical reflection and this optimism must be connected, and therefore that he must resist the relevance of the one because he rejected the grounds for the other. He saw the obvious connection between moral language and the self-interest of nations and groups, and he saw the drastic limits on what a sheer exercise of will can do in the currents of history; therefore, since "morality" has been made to depend on great swatches of freedom and on great abstract universals, and these are gone, then there must not be any point in referring to standards and values in politics.

The realist, like the idealist, confuses these three questions: what is good? what do people think is good? and, what effect do people's ideas about what is good actually have in the situation? There often occurs in their discourse a confusing downward slippage, in which moral questions turn into factual ones, and the whole human activity of evaluation is bypassed to reach the factual issue about how much effect, if any, such evaluation can have upon affairs. Ethical questions keep turning into the historical question of the role of ideas, or of the effect of the will, upon society. There is great use of the word "factor"; "morality" is said to be one factor — a rather pale one — in politics, alongside tanks, banks, and parliaments. One even finds in some policy documents on the national situation, that along after military power and economic power, as one more of the "elements of national power," there comes "faith and ethics." One encounters curious formulations about the "limited" role "morality" can or should play in world politics, as though we want to do some — but not too much! — of what is right. One thinks one is talking about ethics, but all of a sudden one is talking instead about morale, or mores, or popular moral convictions as a sociological fact.

Then there is another, related error shared by realists and idealists alike: they may both accept the picture of "ethics" or "morality" as consisting of absolute laws and rules, of unsullied ideals, and of "pure" motives, devoted exclusively to altruism and opposed completely to coercion. This ethic (taken to be the only ethic) then stands in unmistakable contrast to politics, a realm where relativity and power and compromise are plain and where unaltruistic and coercive behavior do unmistakably appear. Therefore, "ethics" and "politics" or "morality" and "foreign policy" or "morals" and "power" are continually set over against each other.

Mr. Kennan, who wrote in his first book that nations are not a "fit object" for "moral judgment," could write this paragraph in his second book, trying to explain that sentence. Instead he made it clear that his idea of morality is as idealistic, and of politics as dismal, as that of his "moralistic" opponents:

> Morality, then, as the channel to individual self-fulfillment — yes. Morality as the foundation of civic virtue, and accordingly as a condition precedent to successful democracy — yes, morality in government method, as a matter of conscience and preference on the part of our people — yes. But morality as a general criterion for the behavior of states and above all as a criterion for measuring and comparing the behavior of different states — no. Here other criteria, sadder, more limited, more practical, must be allowed to prevail.*

What these other "sadder" criteria are, Mr. Kennan does not say. "Morality," however, is something different from them, and is apparently less "limited" and "practical."

* *Realities of American Foreign Policy* (Princeton, N.J.: Princeton University Press, 1954), page 49. Mr. Kennan also says — I believe, of one of my points — that "the process of government, after all, is a practical exercise and not a moral one" (page 48). That is just the contrast one should not make: Why is not government both?

If Mr. Kennan's idea of morality is as unreal, his idea of politics is also as dismal as that of the moralizers he criticizes. Government, he says, is a "sorry chore"; made necessary — "unfortunately" — by man's irrationality, selfishness, and general nastiness. The word "chore" appears often when government or politics is mentioned; and this "almost embarrassing chore," he wrote, is certainly not the part of undertaking in which such things as "altruism and sacrifice" can find any "pure expression." Mr. Kennan's pen seems here to have slipped into exactly the standard American idea of politics as a black, unfortunate, power-ridden realm. The only changes are that he is inclined to use the word "sorry" instead of "dirty" to describe it, and to hold that it is, regrettably, a necessary activity. To the sorry chore of government, apparently, no ethical considerations apply. The only thing to do is to grit your teeth and go through with it.

I think that a paragraph that Jacques Maritain wrote in correction of Machiavelli may apply also to some realists in contemporary America:

Machiavelli, like many great pessimists, had a somewhat rough and elementary idea of moral science, plainly disregarding its realist, experiential, and existential character, and lifting up to heaven, or rather up to the clouds, an altogether naive morality which obviously cannot be practiced by the sad yet really living and laboring inhabitants of this earth. The man of ethics appears to him as a feeble-minded and disarmed victim, occasionally noxious, of the beautiful rules of some Platonic and separate world of perfection. On the other hand, and because such a morality is essentially a self-satisfying show of pure and lofty shapes — that is, a dreamed-up compensation for our muddy state — Machiavelli constantly slips from the idea of well-doing to the idea of what men admire as well-doing, from moral virtue to appearing and apparent moral virtue; his virtue is a virtue of opinion, self-satisfaction and glory. Accordingly, what he calls vice and evil, and considers to be contrary to virtue and morality, may sometimes be only the authentically moral behavior of a just man engaged in the complexities of human life and of true ethics: for instance, justice itself may call for relentless energy — which is neither vengeance nor cruelty — against wicked and false-hearted enemies. Or the toleration of some existing evil — if there is no furthering of or cooperating with the same — may be required for avoiding a greater evil or for slowing down and progressively reducing this very evil. Or even dissimulation is not always bad faith or knavery. It would not be moral, but foolish, to open up one's heart and inner thoughts to every dull or mischievous fellow. Stupidity is never moral, it is a vice.

In our American case, that beautiful rules Cloudland ethic is around in the environment, and the realists get it from there.

In reacting against idealistic errors while accepting idealistic definitions, the realists may encourage a kind of Hobbesian politics: a power-oriented and interest-oriented interpretation of the political world. Noticing that Americans are peculiarly prone to overlook facts of *power* and *interest,* they underline those notions too heavily, and almost suggest that the whole of politics can be understood through them. They may suggest that one can discover a proper course of action by attending to these two "realities." With respect to power, for example, the respective errors of idealists and realists would go something like this: the idealist makes a negative ethical judgment about power, and idealizes the world to emphasize persuasion and goodwill in place of coercive power. The realist tends to join in the negative judgment but not in the idealizing of the world. Both may leave themselves unable to think explicitly with reference to moral values, when they deal with the political realm in which power is always present. It is especially misleading to amalgamate power and self-interest:

to use a notion of "power" that mixes it with selfishness. To assert the universality of this amalgamation as the central law of politics is then to misconceive "reality" in something of the way the psychological hedonist does (the man, that is, who says all men everywhere always and necessarily seek only their own pleasure). "Power," and "interest," become indiscriminate universals applicable by definition to all behavior from the march of armies to the proclamation of the Atlantic Charter, just as pleasure-seeking in the example covers everything from debauchery to the death of the martyr. Then, further, this leveling indiscriminateness tends to level downwards: when "pleasure," colored by our ordinary limited understanding of it is applied, surprisingly, to that martyr burning at the stake, the effect is to pull him back down into the company of ordinary man; as "power" or "interest," colored by our ordinary use, is made the essence of every political act, the effect may be to make all such acts look just like the worst. Then the further effect may be to justify the worst, since all look alike.

Actually, Mr. Acheson and Mr. Kennan represent in practice, in their differing and at the moment conflicting ways, positions on the morals-and-politics question superior not only to that of their opponents but also to that suggested by these theoretical sentences of their own. Mr. Kennan really is a political moralist in the best sense, bringing a very sensitive system of humane values to bear on world politics. Mr. Acheson has some other sentences that indicate a more adequate position than do those I have quoted. He said he would "state principles in terms of their purpose and effect" rather than in terms of their "morality" or "immorality," and that is fine (because the latter language tends to reflect a legalistic and over-simple moral outlook) so long as one is clear that their "purpose" and "effect" will be related to a standard of value. In politics one should have an evaluating outlook that takes more account of *consequences* (of "purpose" and "effect") than do the law-proclaiming moralizers. Mr. Acheson calls his way the "strategic" approach, and he compares it to the morality of Lincoln rather than that of John Brown, which comparison makes a good point. For further illumination, however, one might look not to these sentences on ethics-and-politics but to the "pattern of responsibility" in Mr. Acheson's own political work.

3. THE AMERICAN MIND AND WORLD REALITIES

1958

One of the early lectures in Mr. Kennan's series on the BBC discussed "the Soviet Mind and World Realities." The world-wide response to his talks suggests that there is an almost equal concern about the *American* mind and world realities. To many Americans, a chief difficulty with proposals for the negotiations, summit meetings, and disengagements is that the Soviets do not think straight, and do not keep their word. They have, in Mr. Kennan's words, "a strange corruption of the mind" on this one subject, the "relationship to any external competitive power." But for much of the world, the Americans seem to have a mental corruption that is strikingly similar: they do not think straight where the Soviet Union is concerned. The remarkable attention paid around the world to Mr. Kennan's lectures came partly from this feeling: it was not so much what he said as that here, at last, was an American who seemed to be free to think imaginatively about "world realities."

The worldwide pressure for negotiation and "disengagement" may have in it a little of an anti-American note on this point. "Negotiation" might almost be said to be the symbol for something larger, a criticism of American "rigidity" in relation to the Communists.

This is not to say that such attitudes are right as, in an excess of self-criticism, a certain type of American idealists sometimes do. The difference between most American and many non-American attitudes toward negotiation and disengagement may reflect greater realism and responsibility on the American side, the by-product of a difference in power and interest. Obviously, America's interests as a great power figure quite differently in the minds of the one and the other: the American community reacts to protect those interests, even at the risk of war; much of the rest of the world is willing, possibly even eager, to see them sacrificed rather than risk war. But in addition, great power itself may have a disciplining effect, making for a sense of responsibility that is missing in those who do not have such power. America may be taking the whole global character of the Communist threat into account with a higher level of seriousness than do those who, not being great powers, react primarily to Communist powers as they figure in a more parochial set of interests. In a sense, other peoples can afford to have illusions about the Soviets and Communism that the United States, the direct and major enemy, cannot risk. For America there is one single overwhelming primary problem embracing the globe: the great power of Russia, China, and the Communist Empire. For the other nations of the world, even for our closest allies, that one problem, great though it is, is necessarily somewhat less central. They do not have the same capacity or responsibility to deal with it. In addition, to some extent, they have another problem. They must cope — even though in very different ways and to quite different degrees — not with one but with two centers of power, vastly greater than their own, which they cannot control, to which they must be responsive, and which hold in their hands, in a new and terrible way, the fate of mankind.

This less powerful, less "responsible" position provides ground for the growth of illusions to which the American power, actually confronting the opponent directly and completely, is not subject.

The primary illusions on the subject of negotiations, in addition to those that have to do with the Soviet Union, are those about the effect of nuclear weapons on international politics. It may be too easily assumed that these weapons create a common overriding worldwide interest in "peace" in the light of which other, conflicting interests become negotiable. But in fact the catastrophic destructiveness of modern war, and the shared interest in avoiding it, do not alter the fundamental difference over the substantive issues — over Eastern Europe and Germany and Formosa — from which war may arise. The desire for "peace" may not be a common interest if each party desires peace only on its own terms and in its own way.

It is surely a mistake to assume that because an accommodation is desirable or even necessary it is therefore possible. It may also be a mistake to assume that it is completely desirable. The extreme advocates of negotiation may believe that "peace" can be the one sole direct aim of policy, and may assume that an accommodation necessarily would be conducive to it; they may also assume that negotiation would almost necessarily result in some accommodation.

One of the most common errors is the assumption that "peaceful" means, like negotiation, necessarily lead to peace; it is the companion of the other assumption, that military means necessarily lead to war. The result of various "means" do not separate out that way. The decisive questions have to do with configurations of power and purpose, and the alteration of the power situation by negotiation might even make war more likely rather than less. A high-level negotiation, like a summit meeting, might arouse hopes which, when disappointed, would sour the atmosphere.

In the insistence upon negotiations a set of images drawn from the ordered patterns and common ethos of individual and national life may be applied too simply to the vastly different realm of international relations. It seems sometimes to be assumed that talks might, as in a debate, persuade the opponent by the sheer force of ideas, or bring into being, in a kind of international brainstorm meeting, some striking ideas not heretofore considered, or, as in a sort of heart-to-heart talk, compose differences by the process of mutual understanding, or, as in a horse trade, give-and-take to everyone's benefit and satisfaction. Negotiation is made too nearly analogous to transactions in personal and national life. The process of negotiation itself is desired, almost without respect to the content or the prospects of the negotiation; the process is separated from the substance because it is too easily assumed that the process itself is a good thing and that the results cannot but be good. If the world did not expect so much from "negotiation" it would be easier to engage in it.

Those with lesser responsibility, believing that some escape from an onerous situation must be available, blame the most responsible power for not discovering it. Some of the negative feelings about the unpleasant reality are attached to the power that must act as the major agent within it. We might draw an analogy to the attitude of domestic nationalist groups to the American Secretary of State: he is always bringing the bad news that the rest of the world exists, that the United States has responsibilities in it, that these responsibilities are costly and risky, and that we cannot have everything the way we want it. A response to this bad news is an antagonism to the Secretary. The criticism of American policy around the world, especially by groups out of power and in nations with little power may reflect some such attitude.

But is this the whole story? Are those who do not have the full burden of power therefore wholly without wisdom about the use of power? Or may they not furnish a needed check upon the limitations of outlook that — along with realism and responsibility — great power may produce? It would be important for Americans to remain open-minded about this.

The peculiarities of American history and culture have produced a certain bias in the way we look at the world, that needs the check and restraint of peoples with a different experience. This check and restraint from others is especially important just because one part of our bias is the innocent assumption that the way we look at the world is self-evidently true, and therefore not in any particular need of criticism. The check and restraint of other cultures is also important, needless to say, because the fate of the world can turn on the nuance of American political understanding. Everybody has a stake in our seeing this thing rightly.

The bias in American attitudes is in an unhistorical or unpolitical view of freedom as a fact. We have a way of seeing the world in voluntary, individual, and moral terms which is a distinct product of our own philosophy and history, and which tends to be excessive. Our primary view of the world is "liberal": the continuities, necessities, and limits of history and society tend to fade away, leaving the unencumbered individual free to choose in an unencumbered present. The liberal emphasis on individual freedom as a *goal* is subtly compounded with an immense emphasis on individual freedom as a fact; we have as little determinism in our make-up as any people ever had. No doubt, on the whole, that is to the good; but it is not without its defects. The defects of the individual and voluntary view are particularly apparent in a field, the corporate conditions of which it overlooks, almost by definition: namely, the field of politics.

The forces of history and culture have conspired to make us so: our material abundance, our physical space, our relative peace and isolation, the relative absence of deep-going national tragedies, have all conduced to a sanguine view of what men can freely do in society. The absence of any feudal past, moreover, meant that economic and political liberalism was in on the ground floor and had no reactionary or revolutionary competitors. Another very important influence was the American religious tradition, with its free church emphasis on the acts and the will of the individual in conversion, revival, and missionary activity. Though much of America's outlook of course is that of liberalism and democracy generally, we carry it much further and give it a distinct coloration; the moralistic, dynamic, and sentimental element that goes beyond liberalism elsewhere, for example, is heavily influenced by the dominant evangelical religious tradition.

From these basic predispositions come not only many American virtues (hopefulness and vitality and an absence of the morbid and defeatist, for example) but also some of the vices to which now the world objects in our attitude towards the Soviet Union.

Our well-known "moralism" grows from this bias, for when one sees the world as one vast open field of freedom, uncomplicated by necessities and limits, then one can move about in it

striking off moral judgments right and left about the way freedom is used. Freedom and moral judgments go together, of
course, and the larger the space you see the former occupying,
the more room you have for exercising the latter. Especially
with reference to Communism and democracy, Americans may
seem to the rest of the world to treat politics altogether too
much in free and moral terms. We seem sometimes to treat
the whole matter as a case of pure choice between obvious
ideological alternatives, a choice which can then be morally
evaluated as right or wrong. We Americans, choosing a self-
evidently right democratic way of life more firmly and unequivocally than other peoples, are therefore by our own implicit
admission righter than anybody; the Communists — the "atheistic" Communists — choosing collectivism and totalitarianism,
are over at the opposite extreme, and are wrong and bad; and
in between on the misty flats the rest drift to and fro.

Neutralism is "immoral" because it is a failure to choose
the clear right against the clear wrong. We often seem to look
upon the struggle as one between righteousness and unrighteousness, good and bad, and upon the nations and peoples of
the world as free, to stand up and be counted in that struggle,
independently of their history, geography, and power position.

American attitudes sometimes suggest that the idea is for
the Communists suddenly to choose to be different. They
suggest also that our attention is focused not upon improvements for the present but upon punishment for the past. Partly
because we are a great power, but more because we are
America, we can allow ourselves the luxury of a moral indignation that lesser powers (who have to trade, say, with Communist China) cannot afford.

It is not that we are in error in our ethical and philosophical
estimate of the behavior of the Soviet Union and of its Com-

munist creed; it is rather that we may make the evil in it too exclusive and unique, and allow that estimate to play a more prominent part in our thought, speech, and policy than it should. It is not that we are wrong about Soviet "unrighteousness"; it is that moral judgments about righteousness and unrighteousness enter too largely into our political calculations. It is not that we are wrong in our principled opposition to the Communist totalitarian internal system and to the behavior of the Communist states; it is rather that questions of "principle" play much too large a role in our estimate of the situation. We may be inclined to underestimate the role of national self-interest and historical necessity in both our own and the Russian action, and to overestimate the role of virtue, principle and choice. The fault is not exactly the moral judgment on the Soviet and Communism, but the unhistorical view in which that judgment is set, a view which tends to make this evil a monolithic and central abstraction, and to assume that because it should be, it therefore can be done away with.

The simpler popular versions of American anti-Communism do not of course characterize American policy-makers, as foreign critics sometimes allege. But they may not be wholly irrelevant, for the public has a large impact on American foreign policy, both in that policy-makers must pay attention to it for external political reasons, and because they are not entirely immune to being affected by it internally. Something of the American view that we can have what we want and can do what is right may spill over even into the sophisticated calculations of policy leaders. Even in their words and acts one may note that other American characteristic, an inclination to confront ourselves with large, absolute rather simple alternatives. This is part of the dichotomous view involved in moralism, and part of the simplicity that democracy tends to produce;

it is also a result of the overlooking of broad factors of power, and the awareness only of overt forms of power. The divorce we are inclined to make between force and policy is part of the larger view that treats power not as integral to all social life but as an extraneous and occasional intrusion. The over-emphasis on freedom-as-fact makes for a strong American resistance to unresolved situations, dilemmas, lesser evils, limits, necessities, inevitabilities. Indeed it seems to us, with our vital, crusading background, dangerous, defeatist, even morally debilitating to admit there are things we cannot do. One of the more dangerous aspects of this is our intolerance toward a situation like the Korean war. It did not make sense to us: either let's win, or get out; either it's war, or it's not. The conception of limited war, as that of limited (that is, historical) objectives which lies behind it, goes against the American grain.

America's inclination toward simple alternatives, excluding subtler political discriminations, seems to make the overt military threat by all means the predominant feature of American understanding of the situation. To much of the world our rather rigid moral opposition to Communism and our rather too simple definition of the struggle may seem to leave us stuck, with nowhere to move except in an ever mounting circle of ever more terrible weapons.

Meanwhile, our moral aims against the Communists are kept intact by declaration and proclamation — by policies of "liberation" the point of which is not to guide or indicate our line of concrete action but to declare the morality of our intent. The trust in and emphasis upon the pronouncement of aspirations and ideals is of course another one of the familiar, outstanding characteristics of American politics; it grows from the habit of getting an emotional lift and from the belief that such hortatory appeals to great ideals, quite apart from the mundane concrete policies in which they may be embodied, can have some powerful effect.

One can understand why, in a period marked by nuclear plenty, such a nation may induce in the lesser powers, dependent upon it for their very life, a touch of nervousness. On the one side they can feel the latent American pull for the simple, clear resolution of a crusading holy war against the evil Communism. On the other side they note the American emphasis on "peace," as though we could have it by declaring for it. Behind them both is a great nation still perhaps not quite domesticated to the trials of politics.

The present pressure for negotiation may reflect the apprehension of the world about these American attitudes. Although they speak of "testing the Russian intentions" they may also want to test, or even to change, the American intentions. They may fear that the Americans have the world so structured into good and evil that they cannot make an adjustment to fact. With the power of nuclear weapons waiting to be used, the most subtle and careful political discriminations must be made but the Americans are not good at such discriminations. Negotiation tends to be regarded by us as an instrument of peace, rather than as one possible part of a larger political process. The Americans at first may have seemed to rule out negotiation not because of the absence of accepted subject, but rather because of our moral disapproval of the opposite party. Negotiation seemed to be predicated on their giving in and reforming, rather than on the situation as it is.

Maybe we have been right to move only reluctantly toward talks with the Russians. But surely we have not been right to create an image of ourselves as unrealistic moralizing power, ready to risk the world's suicide to protect our own preconceptions. The people of the world need to be sure that America can come to terms, if not with the Soviets, at least with history.

4. THE AMERICAN ETHOS AND "FREE WORLD" POLITICS

1959

The United States' new role, as leader of a great "free world" coalition, has requirements that are not exactly congenial to traditional American political and moral attitudes. We Americans are now rather suddenly given a responsibility for which neither our past experience nor our present ideas and values have equipped us very well.

Part of the story is America's long period of noninvolvement in world affairs, but another part of it is the way Americans, for many other reasons, have come to think about the political realm. It is rather as though an invader, more or less out of the system and without experience in the imperial art had suddenly come into control of the Roman Empire.

But America's role in the free world is even more complicated than any such imperial position and more complicated than that of a participant in traditional European balances of power. Just at the time that America has stepped into world responsibilities, the nature of those responsibilities has undergone drastic change. Americans have had to try to learn, simultaneously and in a hurry, both those old things, of traditional diplomatic wisdom, that others knew but she did not, and those new things, like, say, the rules for psychological warfare and economic aid, that nobody knew.

The suddenness with which the United States came into this role has added difficulty to a situation already difficult enough. Less than two centuries after she herself was but a collection of remote colonies, America has become a super-power upon whom all the old colonial powers depend. Less than fifty years after she stepped upon the international stage, in a "splendid little war," she moved to the center of that stage, where wars are no longer little or splendid. Less than ten years after a probable majority of Americans could still support the isolationist side — against all international involvement — in the debate over the events before World War II, the United States was the center of history's most far-reaching set of alliances — and that in peacetime. If Great Britain acquired her empire in a fit of absent-mindedness, the United States acquired her alliance system in a frenzy of activity. In less than ten years after the initial decisions of 1947, the United States had acquired forty-four peacetime allies; most of the alliances, and all the main outlines of the system, were worked out in the mere three years between the Truman Doctrine and the outbreak of the Korean war.

Institutions and attitudes require time to change and develop, but in this case that time has not been granted. We have not had much time in which to develop a diplomatic corps to handle the perennial problems of alliances, or a public to understand them, and we have not had much time, either, to develop the principles, skills, and attitudes, to manage the *new* problems of *this* alliance system. In the same decade we have had to try to develop the ideas, train the people, and shape the institutions, to take on all the old problems of a world power and also all the new ones created, for example, by the economic dimension of the world struggle, by the war for the "minds of men," and by the immense destructiveness of nuclear weapons.

It has obviously had to be a busy time in the practical line.

Along with that, it has had to be a busy time in the intellectual and ethical line, working out a changed understanding of the world and of our responsibilities.

The will of the United States is more dominant than it would be were she but one partner-nation in a company of equals — more even than a first among equals; but at the same time she is far from being an imperial power, ruling by fiat over subordinate peoples. In either of these cases her course would be less difficult, because she would need only to consult her own will and proclaim it. But the United States is not granted the simplification that comes either with unambiguous power over others, or with unambiguous delimitation of responsibility solely to one's own national interest. Instead she has the power and responsibility of the coalition leader, yet she does not have unqualified authority to shape the coalition's policy. The United States is technically one ally in a set of alliances, but actually a superpower with many lesser affiliated powers. She has in fact a large impact on her associates, but she is debarred by her own tradition and the nature of the association from the more blatant impositions of her will.

America is unmistakably the most important maker of decisions in the coalition. This follows in large part from her power and wealth: she is the first and chief nation with nuclear weapons, shielding and allies under her grand deterrent; she is the free world's primary entry in the technological race over space satellites, missiles, nuclear submarines, and the rest; she is the major source of economic aid, loans, technical assistance, from the first loans to Britain in 1947, and the Marshall Plan, down to the continuing foreign aid programs of the present time.

The United States is, actually, the one link holding the whole complex of alliances together; several of the key relations, as with Nationalist China, with Japan, with South Korea, and with the Philippines, are bilateral treaties with the United States; the European, Asian, and South American parts of the whole are not linked except through the United States' membership in NATO, SEATO, OAS, and ANZUS, and through their common dependence on U.S. policy and resources.

It is the United States that bears the central threat and the universal responsibility; other powers, and the lesser ones particularly, relate themselves to the Communist world in their own limited interest and perspective, with less involvement in the global pattern. Pakistan is more worried about India than about China or Russia; France had to be more involved with her own problem in Algeria than with the common problems of the worldwide anti-Communist coalition.

In her own eyes, and also in those of allies, uncommitted nations, and enemies, the United States embodies in a special way the social-economic structure and ideology most directly antipathetic to the Communists: her "capitalism" is purer, her "democracy" more strictly at odds with collectivism, her "American way of life" more thoroughly and aggressively set over against the Communist view. In everyone's eyes she is the Soviets' and the Chinese Communists' number one enemy.

As the principal nuclear power, as the purest capitalist power, as the universally responsible free world power, the United States stands on the front line in this coalition. Where in World War I she could be seen as a power on the periphery, coming in late to the fray to save the day, and where even in World War II she could wait for an unambiguous aggression against herself before entering the war that others already were fighting, by the time of the Korean war no such separate and delayed action was possible. Quite the contrary. Now the United States was the power making the key decision and do–

ing most of the fighting, the front-line power urging others into more active help. Instead of being pulled in, she was doing the pulling.

The Free World is full of tensions, real and potential, which American policy cannot ignore.

The alliance includes both colonial powers and colonies. The United States must hold with those who have, or had, a colonial empire, like England, France, Portugal, and Holland, and must also deal with a large collection of their present or former colonies. She cannot take the unambiguous stand against "colonialism," and for national independence, that some at home and abroad recommend; neither can she stand unqualifiedly beside her European allies in their colonial troubles.

The Free World includes both allies and enemies, from the Second World War. Great Britain and West Germany are two indispensable parts of the North Atlantic alliances, and the United States must mitigate the remaining British antagonisms toward their former enemy, and both adjust to and partly resist the reluctance on the part of some to commit themselves deeply to West Germany's defense. Earlier, she had to press for German rearmament, against peoples with bitter memories.

The coalition includes both democratic states and dictatorships. Not all the states in the alliance, or receiving aid from the United States, have the kind of internal politics about which the democracies can be enthusiastic. The United States often must take what allies it can get; often it must deal with the Rhees, Chiangs, and Titos, with the old South American strong men and new Asian military dictators, not because we like them but because they are there.

The alliance includes both more or less safe states, and more or less endangered states. This classification shifts with the shifting crises of the contest with the Communist power. The pattern, however, repeats itself: those who are immediately threatened or embroiled (Chinese nationalists; South Koreans; West Berliners; Lebanese) want a firm, uncompromising, or aggressive stand when their country is in danger that other, more remote allies and friends may find dangerous, adventuresome, and unnecessary. The United States, to which in every case the conflicting appeals are primarily addressed, must stand in between, mediating and judging the conflicting claims.

Many more conflicts and differences among our allies might be listed, to the same effect: the Asian against the European; the satisfied against the unsatisfied; the non-nuclear against the nuclear. Ancient rivalries and new conflicts play continually within and upon the system, and the United States must constantly act toward parties in dispute. She must work out a solution of the Trieste question between her Italian ally and her Yugoslavian beneficiary; she must deal both with Israel and with Arab nations (allied and non-allied); she must stand with her ally Pakistan but not against the important uncommitted nation of India.

The point about all these struggles is that the United States can neither ignore them nor take one side consistently and unambiguously. She cannot say, as a lesser power might, that the complex Cyprus dispute is not her affair. Neither can she alienate Greeks or Turks or British. She must continually act toward viable compromises and solutions among conflicting friends. As leader she cannot avoid decision, action, and blame; even for not acting and not deciding she is blamed. The whole complicated operation obviously needs the utmost political skill.

Nuclear weapons complicate it further. Their existence greatly increases both the interdependence of nations and the delicacy of their relationship. They obviously raise to un-

precedented heights the stakes resting on key decisions: it may
not be too melodramatic to say that the fate of civilization is
involved. In any case, possibilities of destruction and death
in all nations, quite beyond anything hitherto experienced, are
tied in with the decisions about these weapons and about the
world politics in which they are now a major ingredient.
Everyone's skin may be threatened; every nation's national substance may be endangered. In such a situation there arises a
complex pattern of attraction and repulsion both toward the
weapons and toward the chief allied nuclear power. A nation
may be attracted toward a nuclear development of its own,
as in France's case, not only because nuclear weapons mean
power, honor, and a fuller sovereignty in general in our time,
but also because in particular a nation so equipped can now
itself make the decision, to defend itself with these weapons,
and to pull its allies into the fight. But there is also a repulsion
toward having nuclear weapons, and thus making oneself a
potential target for the enemy's nuclear strike. Similarly, there
is a twofold worry about American decisions and nuclear
weapons: a worry that their suicidal destructiveness will cause
the Americans not to strike when one's own nation is attacked;
a worry that the Americans will use them too precipitately in
some other case in which one's own vital interest is not involved. The inter-allied discussion of these matters necessarily
reflects, discreetly, subtly, in muted tones, something of a
pristine ethical situation: each one desiring to save himself, but
each also desiring to include the others in his own fight; each
desiring that someone else take the greater risks.

Nuclear weapons also necessitate a discriminating policy
in that they make absolute decisions catastrophic, and require
the ability to relate force to policy in the most careful way.
Sheer power no longer is decisive; the psychological release

of all-out war no longer is an acceptable alternative. Instead, objectives must be carefully limited and measured, "costs" of policies carefully assessed, the use and threat of force carefully related to discriminating analysis of Communist intentions, of allied convictions, and of our own purposes.

We Americans are not oversupplied with the wisdom our situation requires. Perhaps the indictments of our approach — of our "escape from politics" — have not sufficiently given credit for the adaption Americans *have* made to the new international responsibility; perhaps the indictments sometimes imply that this country should somehow exhibit a degree of political sophistication never seen on land or sea. Probably the faults that are listed are not exclusively American, and probably there are unnoted virtues mixed in with those faults. Nevertheless, there is truth in the indictment.

One can understand how Americans came to have *their* characteristic ways of fleeing politics (which are not necessarily more marked or worse than the ways in which other peoples may do the same). Both historical conditions and ideas played a role. Among the former, one could list the long period of relative idolization; the absence of the deepest kinds of national tragedy — defeat in war, for example; the success and continuity of the political system; the building of an economy of abundance, that could bypass, with increased production, problems of scarcity with which other nations have to struggle; the absence of the remnants of the feudal order, such as the more fundamental class divisions. Our ideas tend in the same direction: the individualistic ideas of the classical liberal creed; the empiricism that wants all the facts and certainty; the puritan and sectarian tradition that wants clear moral lines and the individual's change of heart. These influences incline us to underestimate the collective base of life, in this nation overwhelmingly dedicated to "individualism," to overlook the pervasiveness of power, in this nation trusting mightily in moral exhortation and majority votes; to underestimate the impact of interest on the minds and actions of men and nations; and to overestimate the harmony that is actual and possible among those interests. Americans tend to make a simple transfer from the more exact field of technique, in which they excel, to the inexact world of politics, in which they do not. They have a hard time living with imponderables, and with unresolved situations.

The nonpolitical American coloration that results affects the outlook of both conservatives and liberals, of both internationalists and nationalists.

At the outset of the containment policy and the beginning of the building of the "free world" alliances, in 1947, there were the two opposite strands of criticism, the more internationalist and the more nationalist.

For the more thoroughgoing internationalist, the collective self-defense system has appeared to be an impure thing, a compromise, a renewal of the old, evil "power politics." It appeared to be a direct contrast to the universal collective security program of the United Nations. Internationalists of this stripe protested against the Truman Doctrine in 1947; some (though by no means all) participated in the Wallace protest of 1947–1948; they objected to the creation of NATO; they continue to protest against "bypassing the UN" today. Many have believed, moreover, that a world government is now possible. The United Nations may represent to them something of the inclusiveness and something of the rule of law that they desire, but not as fully as they would like. The collective self-defense system (NATO) is quite another matter. It is particular, not universal; it is directed against a specific enemy, not against aggression in general; it is obviously motivated more by self-interest and self-protection than by a disinterested attachment to a principle; it includes a prominent military element. Therefore, it is an undesirable thing.

The nationalists also have been disgruntled by the free world coalition, but for different reasons. One continuing expression of the American attitude we have described is a kind of cocky unilateralism, a feeling that we can do what we want and that we should "go it alone." This American nationalism has in it elements that mark that phenomenon everywhere: a strong, sensitive sense of the nation's honor and glory; a certain xenophobia; a love of display of the nation's power. In addition, the American version is more affected than most by a strong sense of national separation, uniqueness, freedom, and power. The same spirit could support, in one moment, the isolationist alternative, too much withdrawn (non-intervention before World War II, Herbert Hoover's "Fortress America" in the "great debate" in 1950) and in another moment an adventurous, expansive semi-imperialist policy, too little restrained (unconditional surrender, the "American Century," General MacArthur's expansionistic impulses). A common denominator of the apparently contradictory policies is the desire to exercise an unsullied and untrammeled national will. The nationalist spirit is restive with real allies, because they obviously place restraints upon us. Mixed in with that is a dislike of the foreigner, anyway. Usually, too, the nationalist wing is the more blatantly anti-Communist and pugnacious, inclining more toward preventive war and surer of our unbeatable strength; allies appear to be unnecessary and restrictive, and also somewhat soft and weak-willed in the contest with the Communist power.

These two extremes, tending for contrary reasons to oppose

the coalition, actually have some underlying attitudes in common. They share the uncalculating neglect of the specific correlation of forces in the real world — the one by consulting
only its ideals, the other by consulting only its image of the
national glory. They share a desire that the nation act in a
single "pure" way, rather than on a mixed and compromised
course, acting partly in response to allied needs and pressures.
They share the desire to resolve by some decisive act the unresolved problems of history.

Now the relation of attitudes to the alliance is more refined.
The struggle concerns aspects of the alliance rather than its
whole justification. Part of the dispute deals with preferences
among allies. Just as different allies disapprove of each other,
so different factions approve and disapprove of different sets
of allies. The more internationalist persuasion, accommodated
in part to a collective defense system, may nevertheless find
repugnant the dictatorships and "reactionary" regimes attached
to it. The alliance, in their view, should have a purer ideological content. Some members of the so-called "free-world," said
one complaint, are in no sense "free." In such a complaint
there is too much ideology and too little realization of the
limits on the power and freedom of the United States. There
is too little recognition that the alliance must be based not so
much on compatibility of social structures as on a common
interest in resisting the Communist empire. At least some
justification for the term "free" can be found in the common
desire for freedom from Soviet control, and some understanding of the need for "impure" allies in the measures necessary
to defend that freedom.

But if the internationalist has disapproved of Franco and
Chiang and Rhee and South American dictators and Arab po-
tentates, and maybe sometimes of Adenauer, the nationalist

has preferred these very allies to others who in his view are less staunchly anti-Communist. His implicit tests are not only solid anti-Communism, but also pro-Americanism, and strength. England and France may sometimes appear to him to be too "soft" in regard to the common enemy; certainly the courting of India, and of other uncommitted nations of Southeast Asia, does not appeal to him. Really, he too has an ideological way of testing our allies and friends.

Similar patterns of principled opposition appear also in regard to other questions of the conduct of the alliance. They appear, for example, when we consider the relative weight of our own national will and the relative merit of our own unilateral action, as against those of our allies. Some internationalists have an automatic and principled preference for collective action, the more collective the better. Action "through the UN," in this view is always morally preferable to action through NATO or other alliances, and then, in turn, action with allies is automatically preferable to unilateral action. There is an ethical presumption in favor of action by collective international agencies which too easily assumes that collectivity in itself is necessarily a good.

One may say that the free world system is justified from the realistic side too much in terms of national interest, and from the idealist side too much in terms of collectivity as a good. The important judgment rests with the justice of the cause itself, rather than whether it is pursued multilaterally or unilaterally.

Similarly, the principled American internationalist may overvalue the opinions of allies, or uncommitted powers, as against the conclusions of his own government: how Indians and other Asians feel, or sometimes how the English and French feel, can too automatically be given first place. Some residual wis-

dom is thought to be there, some disinterested insight, that is
not available over here. This appears especially with reference
not to governmental opinion in the nations in question, but to
popular opinion; the allied publics are part of that "world
public opinion" to which frequent appeal is made. On the
other hand, the nationalist might seem almost to make it a
principle never to consider seriously the opinions of the others,
but to go ahead in our own way.

With reference to the conduct of the alliance there is a
similar division concerning the military and economic-political
aspects respectively. Some idealists too automatically prefer
economic "aid" to military, and some realists the reverse. Both
have their rather *a priori* estimates of what is needed and of
what both Americans and allies really want. The discussion
over what to *call* our aid, for the purpose of congressional action and popular support, is an interesting case in point. Some
held that congressmen and other Americans are more likely
to approve military than economic aid; therefore, the phrase
and category of "defense support" was devised, to include some
essentially non-military items under this military rubric. Others
have held, however, that the reverse is true: more aid ought
to be given and administered as economic aid. Some go further, and want as much foreign aid as possible divorced not
only from military considerations but from any policy considerations whatsoever: it should be taken away, not only from
the Defense Department, but even from the State Department,
and made something like a disinterested outpouring of benefi-
cence.

One way to summarize is to say that we Americans seek
and presuppose — as internationalists and nationalists, conservatives and liberals — a *purer* action — a pure disinterested-
ness, or a pure national act, in a pure solution that finally re-

solves the ambiguities and limitations of history — than is
feasible in world politics.

5. THE RIGHT ANSWERS TO THE WRONG QUESTIONS
January, 1958

At a recent conference on "ethics and nuclear weapons" a
moral theologian established succinctly and precisely, on the
basis of Catholic teachings, that nuclear weapons are immoral.
He alluded to the historic teaching that, in the course of a just
war, it may be necessary incidentally to cause the death of innocent persons, but he did not find in this sufficient justification for the use of major nuclear weapons.

The multiple evils involved in the nuclear bombing of a
great city like Moscow or New York, he pointed out, would be
so immense, so incalculable, so central to the act itself, so certain and real, that one could not justify them as an incidental
side result that one would "permit" as a secondary effect of the
achieving of some overriding "good" (even the defeat of or
reprisal against Communist Russia). Rather than commit this
evil act a nation should "abandon itself to Divine Providence."
Nuclear weapons, said the moralist, are immoral. And he sat
down.

This talk illustrates both the perennial problem of ethics
and politics, and the dramatic exaggeration of that problem
in the nuclear age. Cogent in its own terms, the speech nevertheless seemed irrelevant to the larger scene. Some other
presentations by morally earnest folk seem less cogent and
equally irrelevant; they are more or less compelling answers
to unasked questions. This is the danger we all feel in the
ethical discussion of political questions: that we be led by con-

centrating on "morality" to give the right answers to the wrong
questions, and the wrong answers to the right questions. Our
correct conclusion to a narrowly conceived ethical question
may lead to a mistaken attitude toward the broader field of
political choices.

In the case of nuclear weapons, the question the times presents is not exactly whether nuclear bombardment of innocent
urban masses, or the effect of radioactivity and genetic de-
terioration on humanity, are evil in themselves; obviously they
are, and, at the extreme of all-out nuclear war, they are horribly
so. The question is not whether, taken by itself, it would be
better that we stop nuclear tests, or that we cease manufac-
ture of nuclear weapons. Obviously, if there were nothing else
to consider, it would be. But the question we really are stuck
with is, given the plentiful and growing existence of the weapons, the danger of nuclear war, the antagonism and expansive-
ness of Communist power, and the worldwide responsibilities
of the United States, what are we to do?

The problem is not a simple, abstract moral issue, but a constant, complicated, political-and-moral situation. For the moral
consciousness to make connection with "the art of the possible"
it must pay attention to what *is* possible. That probably does
not include a nation's abandoning itself to Divine Providence
in the face of the Russian missiles.

Ethics and politics are in a constant, ironic tension, because
while political decisions tend to have consequences that vastly
outweigh the neat individual moral puzzles in the ethics text-
book, and to have mammoth ethical significance (the life,
death, employment, starvation, happiness, misery, freedom,
slavery, of millions of "innocent" humanity near, far, born and
unborn, and the state of whole civilizations), the attempt to
deal with these decisions in "moral" terms nevertheless tends

not only to be irrelevant but even ethically misleading. The biggest ethical questions are the least amenable to purely "ethical" treatment. The right thing in politics is rarely done by the man who tries too intently to do "right"; the moral acts are seldom those suggested by spokesmen who strive explicitly to be "moral."

The moral consciousness, particularly as it has developed in the euphoric American atmosphere, runs toward absolute distinctions of right and wrong, separated out of the historical-political context, divorced from other, possibly contradictory but less dramatic considerations, excluding the moral worth of the self-interest of collectives like the nation, and (most of all) inadequately attentive to the consequences in a particular political situation of a moral conclusion. The moral consciousness drives either toward implicitly assuming that the conditions exist for the realization of its claims or toward saying "no matter what" and "here I stand, God help me, I can do no other" and "do justice though the heavens fall."

But neither assuming that collective altruism is a simple possibility nor striking a "no-matter-what-here-I-stand" posture is ordinarily a good move for a statesman, or for a citizen in his political role. In politics, where men act not just for themselves but for others, the problem is not to say what would be desirable if collective man were good but rather what can be done in the light of the fact that he is not, and the problem is precisely to do as much justice as can be done *without* allowing the heavens to fall.

There is a note of irresponsibility, a subterranean drive toward the luxury of a pure conscience and the satisfying exhilaration of a clear moral stand in much of our desire to make dramatic and absolute denunciations of evils like those associated with nuclear weapons. Such denunciations tend toward a premature moral heroism. The problem *now* is not to decide what to do in the extreme situation, but rather to find ways to prevent that situation from coming about.

The moral theologian at the conference was asked what, having concluded that *using* nuclear weapons was immoral, he would say about *manufacturing* and *threatening* to use them. He blinked as though the question were absurd, and said that of course it was also immoral to *make, have,* and *threaten to* use them. But though that answer may make sense in a strictly formal ethical discourse, it doesn't connect with reality very well. We threaten implicitly and explicitly to use nuclear weapons not only because this may prevent their use against us but also in order that the threat of them now may prevent the situation from arising one day in which we would use them again ourselves. To abandon our program of nuclear weapons would of course be a catastrophic move not only for ourselves but also for all our allies who depend for defense upon the threat of our nuclear retaliatory power; abandoning ourselves to Divine Providence would also mean abandoning, on our decision, many other nations, too.

Ethical reflection concerned with political issues, but divorced from concrete political conditions, may even lead to attitudes and decisions that, quite contrary to their own intent, are unethical in result.

All this is not to say, as the Machiavellian political tradition has tended to do, that ethical considerations are and should be wholly irrelevant or subordinate to political considerations, the Prince learning to do good or not to do good according to the needs of the hour. It is rather to say that a knowledge of the needs of the hour is indispensable to knowing what it is to do good.

If we grant the importance of beginning with the political

context, then ethics no longer needs to be the irrelevant voice from another planet, nor a minor aspect of policy only occasionally to be considered, but rather an angle from which the whole can be viewed and criticized. Ethics then is not the application of pre-existent abstract laws but the critical inquiry into existing reality. The criticism must of course proceed from ethical assumptions but the effort explicitly to spell out these assumptions (laws, values) and then to "apply" them to reality often leads to a dreadful foreshortening of the ethical assumptions and a misreading of the reality. It is usually better, in political ethics, that a man apply himself critically to a concrete situation than that he apply a law or principle deductively to a theoretical problem.

This is peculiarly important in relation to American policy and nuclear weapons. Americans have a penchant for confronting themselves with absolute choices; they tend to ask that the world yield clear, certain, unequivocal results that the world is notably disinclined to furnish.

We have grave difficulty in living under the knife, in tolerating an unresolved situation, in choosing the lesser of evils, in taking risks without certainty of a clear result. Our happy history and our optimistic practical temper have made us insist that results *can* be achieved, problems *can* be solved; nothing is more annoying to the authentic American than the suggestion that there are limits to what we can do. We have the "know-how" for everything.

This inclination, springing in part from our practicality, is reinforced by our moralism. The American religious community bears a considerable responsibility for it, and it is a threat in the nuclear age. One might even go so far as to say we Americans are more dangerous with nuclear weapons than the Russians. Why? Because our practicality and moralism join to make a kind of double-or-nothing psychology, and double-or-nothing is a frightening game with nuclear weapons.

The moralistic part of that psychology works like this: it makes very rosy assumptions about the essential harmony among men and nations and about what can be accomplished by persuasion and good will; therefore the instruments of power appear unnecessary and evil in themselves. All politics seems nasty, but international "power politics," with its alliances, coalitions, armaments, and balances of power, seems especially so.

Most unnecessary and evil of all is the resort to war. The way to prevent war is not to maintain a balance of power, but rather to denounce war and renounce its instruments. The way to be anti-war is to be anti-military, and to oppose "power politics."

In peacetime the representatives of this frame of mind oppose measures of military preparedness and of alliance. But then when war comes, force has been made so evil that no psychological and moral restraints upon its use have been developed; war has been pictured as such an utter catastrophe, such a complete break from normal life, that it is another, awful, world, discontinuous with this, an interruption or parenthesis in history's course.

While we are in that other world, anything goes. Ironically, the idealist and the militarist join in creating the mindset that believes that "in war there is no substitute for victory." And since that world of war and force is utterly evil, entering it can only be justified by the highest, most sweeping (and most uncompromising!) moral ideals. Thus at the extreme it might even be charged that American idealism not only helps to bring on the wars it condemns but also may make them worse when they come.

Our American inclination can be seen in the spirit with which we have responded in the past; one week World War I was none of our business, the next week it was a war to end war and make the world safe for democracy. We were isolationist before World War II, failing to oppose the expansion of the totalitarian powers, then when war came we fought for "unconditional surrender." The Korean war was the most recent and most exact example of this American consciousness; as the war went on the American people became increasingly frustrated with it, and politicians capitalized on the frustration. The feeling was exactly the one we have been identifying and criticizing; let's have a clear resolution. Let's either win this war or get out. Let's fish or cut bait.

Most of us can remember the secret, sneaking joy of release that came when a long anticipated entry into war, like that in World War II, finally came. At least, now we knew where we were; we knew what the goal was, and we could organize all our energies toward it.

We are now in a prewar situation again. Our moral idealism may again build toward such an eventual release by the absolute and catastrophic way in which it treats the nuclear world. But a morality of denunciation, absoluteness, and anti-politics, is misplaced; what we need in the time of the absolute weapon is not an absolute but a highly discriminating ethic; what we need is not one sharp line, but the ability to draw many lines; what we need is the moral stamina to prepare now to avoid, and to resist to the end, the absolute psychological release.

If the moral theologian ended on the wrong note, at least he spoke out of the right tradition, the tradition of the careful distinctions of the just war. It may seem anomalous to speak of a "just war" in the age of weapons that can destroy civilization, but, really, it is in such an age that we need to bring force

under the control of limited objectives, so that the force itself
can be limited. We need to prepare now to give ourselves the
maximum number of choices short of all-out war.

The program for possible "limited war" that Henry Kissinger
and others write about would make heavy moral demands upon
us: demands that we support a more varied military capacity
than our present dependence on nuclear weapons, demands
that we engage in a more imaginative, flexible, and discriminating diplomacy than "massive retaliation," demands that we
be able to sustain for the long haul the unresolved contest, perhaps including sometimes limited military contests, with the
Communist world.

Perhaps the real ethical test of the present is not that of the
degree of our horror at the bomb but that of the energy and
imagination with which we meet those demands.

6. WHICH UNTHINKABLE THOUGHTS DO WE THINK?
April, 1961

The center of Herman Kahn's influential book *On Thermonuclear War* is the insistence that we must think about that subject. Certainly we should, but how? Not only as strategists,
but as men.

Mr. Kahn makes many critical remarks about the naïveté and
irresponsibility with which his subject has hitherto been treated.
"Why don't we care?" he asks, and, typically, answers with a
list or rather, with several lists.

It is true that many of us have difficulty confronting the
possibilities of a world in which five million or twenty million or
eighty million or one hundred and sixty million persons have
been killed. It is true that many of us have not precisely

analyzed the differences among these worlds: their different "acceptability," the different lengths of time it would take to recover, and so on (one of Mr. Kahn's main points is that our preparation could make large changes in these matters). It is true that most of us have not gone into detail about life (or whatever it would be) under such conditions.

It may be true that many of us have elements of what he very often and contemptuously refers to as "wishful thinking." No doubt it is true that more thought should be given to the problems of force and politics in the thermonuclear age than has so far been given. Mr. Kahn is quite right that there are many non-military folk — "utopians," he calls them — who do not like, and do not examine, military problems. Perhaps Mr. Kahn is to be commended, as the statements on the jacket and in some reviews have commended him, for resolutely and even jauntily advancing over into the territory of thermonuclear devastation, to analyze its parts and possibilities in discriminate detail. But there is another side to the matter. Thermonuclear war is too important a subject to be left to the game-theorists.

These remarks are not intended to be a "review" of this book, which I would not be technically competent to review. (Part of the problem about the whole field rests there, by the way). What I want to do, rather, is to comment on the world of thought, or "analysis," out of which the book comes, and which it intends to promote in the leadership and populace, and also to suggest that such a study of thermonuclear war should be combined with equally bold and thorough studies of other aspects of our unprecedented situation.

Mr. Kahn, who has a curiously chatty and digressing and jazzy style — even for lectures, as these originally were — writes many paragraphs about the way committees think, and the way particular groups of people think ("intellectuals"; "bureaucrats"; "idealists"), and many spot analyses of the reasons why we and they think so. Perhaps we can be forgiven, therefore, if we comment not on the substance but on the method and manner of his book — on the way *his* kind of people think. The substance, anyway, is impossibly complicated (in one of his chatty asides he explains that we have to be "at least" this complicated, and that we should be savagely critical of those who are less so). And the foreword states that the book is as remarkable for its method as for its conclusions.

That method seems to me to have grave deficiencies as well as a certain necessary utility. My belief is that it should be more self-critical than it is, and more subordinate than it is. The thought-world from which the book comes is that of the technical-mathematical treatment of social problems — the approach that treats human society as though it were a machine, and makes quantitative calculations about the way it works.

This approach can yield important knowledge, but at the highest moral and philosophical level, of course, it is fatally defective. Its practitioners often do not know when they have moved to that level; instead, the language and method and assumptions needed for "analytical" and mathematical work often bootleg in an ethic and a metaphysic of a dubious sort. Also, style and taste are important when we are dealing with the extremes of human life and death; behavioristic analyses characteristically are not strong in these regards.

These considerations about what is implied in a method and a style, reach their highest intensity when we deal with the humanly-initiated destruction of millions, of civilization, even of human life, that may be involved in a modern war. A certain awe — to put it mildly — should surround our contemplation of such matters. A certain sensitivity should attend our discussion of them. It is true that even on such problems careful, precise, impersonal, technical analysis has to be done somewhere — but it should not dominate, it should not set the tone for, the entire consideration. And it should not then be set forth in jazz-talk.

It is illuminating to note the nervous sentence in the foreword by Klaus Knorr: ". . . though the subject matter raises profound moral problems, this is not a book about the moral aspects of military problems."

Bernard Shaw points out in the preface to *Saint Joan* that ecclesiastics, by constantly handling holy things, become insensitive to holiness. The analogy is not right, but it makes my point to say that military planners, by constantly dealing with destruction, may become insensitive to its larger human meaning.

There are two sides to this, of course. Laymen who overhear doctors jocularly talking about their mistakes, or who overhear politicians making cynically "political" remarks, may be unduly shocked, failing to recognize that there are moral discriminations built into the profession, taken for granted by practitioners despite their unbuttoned, shorthand conversation. Similarly, there is often an unjustified layman's reaction against the language of military strategy, especially in the nuclear age, that quite unfairly attributes callousness to the participants. There sometimes is, in fact, a kind of bearer-of-bad-tidings effect in a naïve reaction against writers like Henry Kissinger and Herman Kahn; it blames them somehow for the world they discuss, as though Mr. Kissinger were positively in favor of having a limited war, and Mr. Kahn responsible for a thermonuclear war.

Such a reaction is, of course, absurd. Against it one must maintain that in this field as in others the professional, because of his superior knowledge of detail, may make important moral discriminations (even though not in "moral" language) that the layman misses. One might argue that Mr. Kahn's effort to persuade us to build shelters, and otherwise increase preparations both for avoiding and for surviving thermonuclear war, falls in that category. The professional's superior knowledge of the hard facts may make him face up to real moral requirements the layman tries to dodge.

But all this applies only *within* a discipline, and not with respect to the unexamined assumptions upon which it proceeds. Where the subject has problems and dubious aspects in its very nature the technician in the field characteristically is blind. There the layman, or outsider, or generalist, may have something to say. The less professional, the more "technical" (impersonal, "objective," quantitative) the field of thought, and the broader its social consequences, the more it requires ethical criticism from beyond its own frame. Military strategy, with these weapons, both has immense social consequences and — in the hands of Herman Kahn — is a very "technical" affair. Therefore, treatments like his badly need the corrective and criticism of a larger frame, in which military strategy is subordinate to politics and politics connected to ethics, in a human and humane rather than a mathematical language.

For Mr. Kahn, paradoxically, it is necessary to convince us that thermonuclear war is quite possible in order to make us take the steps that are most likely to prevent it. He does not enough admit the simpler possibility, that by making thermonuclear war seem thinkable and survival possible one may make thermonuclear war more likely. The tender-mindedness he wishes to overcome may be a basic moral revulsion that should not be overcome.

Let us give an example of the desirable style and approach to the largest contemporary international problems: the style and approach of George Kennan. On specific points and positions, one may of course disagree with him, but on the matters I am discussing — style and method — Mr. Kennan, who is a kind of moralist, represents what we need in thinkers about thermonuclear war. He writes sentences carefully. He is aware of his limitations as a man, and continually indicates that awareness in a tentative and personal element in his style. He combines ethical sensitivity with political and technical knowledge, and makes the latter subordinate to the former. His historical wisdom is primary, his technical calculations secondary. He thinks what the words he is writing mean in real and human terms. One never fears that he will turn himself into a computer.

Now, the other point I want to make is that Mr. Kahn's bold approach to thermonuclear war — that it is survivable, "thinkable," plan-for-able, maybe even do-able — requires equal boldness in other directions. A thermonuclear war, even with Mr. Kahn's shelters, would be a major catastrophe (I trust Mr. Kahn would allow that phrase, even though it is inexact). If we are to plan for it, and think about it (as we should), we should equally boldly think about and plan for other radical developments and courses of action, for example in disarmament, in tacit agreements to co-exist, in losing the struggle, in making international economic ventures. Destruction on the scale Mr. Kahn is talking about is a deep historical event that changes all the possibilities, in unforeseeable ways; yet Mr. Kahn treats everything except that war in quite conventional terms. Nation-states are still fighting for their interests, the larger "GNP" and the ranch house economy is still much desired, the international ideological opposition is undiminished, and so on.

To treat a possible event of the depth and magnitude of

thermonuclear war therefore requires a profound historical imagination, a playing on the possibilities in every direction, and an acute moral sense. Mr. Kahn, consequently, is surely right when he says that we need the thought of persons outside military strategy and mathematical calculation to deal with world politics in our strange era.

7. WEAPONS IN THE WEB OF POLITICS
January 18, 1962

Much of the material by religious folk on morality and nuclear war treats the subject, understandably, in tones of outrage, exhortation, and wild hope: "Fifteen years in hell is enough!" "Britain could save the world by completely disarming herself, and thus, by a blazing act of faith, abolish war." "It is now high time for men to tell the politicians: we do not want mankind to embark upon annihilating itself." But though we can certainly understand why this note is struck, and though of course it is much superior to the appalling so-called "Christian anti-Communism" over on the Right, still it does not touch and stir and move the reader — at least not this one — in the way that it obviously is intended to.

Why not? Not only because its themes are now clichés but also because, even before they were clichés, they lacked a real connection with the main elements and necessities of the matter. Material in this vein tends to treat nuclear arms apart from the web of problems with which they are intertwined in their real political setting; it tends to imply that, just by an act of will, we could leap out of that web — leaving behind the network of obligations represented by our alliances, the threat of an expansive world-wide Communism empire, and the limits on what one can expect a government and a people to be persuaded to do. Sometimes, too, in these tracts there is a scolding scorn for "politicians," implying that they are morally obtuse, that is not at all convincing; some "politicians" may really have a better grip on the goods and evils of the matter, because they are directly involved in it, than do many spiritual counselors. A few sober pages in Henry Kissinger's *Nuclear War and Foreign Policy* dealing with the impact of a nuclear strike on the interdependent life of a modern city may more effectively touch the reader's moral sensitivity and make more vivid to his imagination and conscience what a nuclear war could mean than can the proclamatory statements by many nuclear pacifists.

But by no means all religious reflection on this subject is of that character. *War and the Christian Conscience* by Paul Ramsey, who teaches in the department of religion at Princeton, consists of vigorous and thorough argument rather than exhortation and lament. Moreover, it deals quite insistently not with the destructive consequences of the weapons but rather with the principles of their use; it sorts out and underlines a point which may get lost and which the moralist is peculiarly charged to find again — namely, the point about the evil that *we* may commit. So much of the talk on nuclear war deals with the possible destructiveness for all concerned, and especially for our side, that we may overlook this other aspect of the thing: the death and destruction that we may cause by our own act. There is a distinct question, one that should not be smothered by reference to the Russians, about our own deeds, tested against our own ideas of what it is right for a nation to do. Mr. Ramsey deals with that question.

Although his book defends a position not many in the end will accept, there is nevertheless an energetic and persistent moral intelligence moving through it that gives it strength and forces the reader to attend to its point. The point is that only "counter-forces" and not "counter-peoples" war is justifiable. But stating it baldly will not bring out its full meaning. It grows out of a series of interwoven and carefully reasoned arguments.

The fundamental argument has to do with the way one thinks about moral questions. Mr. Ramsey argues against the "future-facing" moral outlook that "reduces" ethical thinking merely to calculations of better and worse results; he speaks in the language of all those defenders of principle, duty, and moral law who resist making morality simply a matter of quantities, sizes, proportions, and numbers. He presses this general point not only against the compromises of the "realists" but also against the arguments of the "no-greater-evil" nuclear pacifists, who in their own way speak too much about good or (mostly) bad results, rather than about right and wrong. Mr. Ramsey insists that morality deals first of all with conduct, with the form of right action, with the lawful and the unlawful. You must deal with what is right and (more especially) wrong — what is out of bounds — before you begin calculating degrees of good or evil. You have to set the boundaries beyond which you simply say "No" before you begin talking about greatest good for greatest number and all that. Mr. Ramsey disagrees with many of his fellow Protestant moralists because he thinks that they have made Christian ethics too "prudential" or "realistic," losing the solid general rules for right action in calculations about contingencies and consequences.

This apparently abstract ethical discussion has point because Mr. Ramsey argues for a *principle* with respect to nuclear weapons. He takes what many would have regarded the most

outdated part of the generally outdated classical theory of the
"just war" — the requirement that war be conducted with "just
means" — and applies it firmly to the military situation of our
own time: force may be "just" when directed at an opposing
force, but it cannot be just when directed at great masses of
people.

This principle is not something Mr. Ramsey just thought up
on his own; it comes from the great fund of moral wisdom built
into the arduously worked-out classical Christian discriminations and requirements of the just war — or rather the "justifiable" — war. All this, one might argue, should not be thrown
aside, but rather should be all the more clearly and firmly
pressed now that modern technology makes unlimited destruction possible, and modern ideology makes nations all the more
prone to ignore any limits on the use of force. Mr. Ramsey,
following the Catholic moralist Father John Ford, finds in this
ancient tradition of the natural law of justice of war a principle
that we should now use to limit force: the principle of just
means. The evil of the bombardment of cities is so direct,
"intended," and certain that it cannot be justified, as other killing in war may be, as a tragically necessary side effect. The
giant weapons are wrong for the same reason that obliteration
bombing was wrong: they bring the indiscriminate, ungoverned destruction of people. The moral line to be drawn is
not that between force and no force, or war and peace, as
pacifists claim; nor between nuclear bombs and "conventional"
force, as some moderns assert. The line, rather, should be
drawn between the limited resistance to an opponent's force
and the ungoverned, violent destruction of peoples.

This position obviously involves holding to one more traditional notion that many will think utterly passé: the traditional notion of the immunity of noncombatants. To those who

hold that such a requirement is a now fantastic remnant of a long-past chivalric notion of war, quite out of place in the age of modern total war, Mr. Ramsey and Father Ford would reply: so much the worse for modern war. War is not — nor ever should be — "total" in the sense that every man, woman, and child is a legitimate target. The subjective "innocence" of draftees as against civilians is not the point, but rather the objective participation in a force — a clear and present danger — that may and must be resisted. The soldier, whatever his state of mind and motive and however he got there, is part of this force; wives and barbers and schoolchildren are not. True, war regularly involves the incidental killing of some noncombatants, but that is a different thing from direct bombing of mass populations. Of course neat lines cannot be drawn, but that does not mean that we cannot distinguish the extremes. To resist an "unjust" attacker's army and military engine is legitimate; to attack his people indiscriminately is not. To resist an assailant's attack is legitimate; to threaten his wife and children to make him desist is not. The latter, says Mr. Ramsey, is what we are now doing: for our political purpose, we are threatening the lives of thousands of Moscow schoolchildren. That act is unjustifiable.

What then would he have us do? Disarm and rearm. He follows former AEC Commissioner Thomas Murray in saying that we should try a one-at-a-time dismantling of the megaton weapons, pressing the Russians to reciprocate. Even if they do not, we should dispose of these immoral, undiscriminating, "unusable" terror weapons, and rearm with usable and limited force — force that is rational and morally justifiable.

Certain rebuttals to Mr. Ramsey's argument are obvious enough. First, one would have to disagree with him about the method of ethics appropriate to politics; reflection about what

ought to be done in national policy must take primary account-
ing of consequences and of possibilities in a particular setting.
Although we have principles, we have several that conflict, not
just one that settles the matter absolutely even before we look
at the situation. Although his argument is much superior to
most in this direction, in the end Mr. Ramsey is like many
idealistic writers in abstracting nuclear arms from their political setting. Putting them back in that setting, one would have
to argue that continuing to possess the larger ones as a deterrent is not "useless, irrational terror" but does have use: it may
help prevent the evils that would ensue if they were possessed
by the other side only — the evils, that is, of the intimidation
of the world by the Communist power. Khrushchev's indelicate
remarks about fifty-megaton and hundred-megaton bombs, and
his intimations at the time of the Suez and Cuban affairs, along
with much more evidence, make it clear that such evils are not
fanciful. Not only our own but the schoolchildren of allies
and the non-Communist peoples have a kind of protection,
real though very precarious, under the umbrella of that posses-
sion. For the moment it helps to maintain a dangerous but
real international order. The principled unilateral rejection of
the H-bomb, in the inconceivable event that national leaders
should adopt it, would bring desperate and unpredictable consequences. It would not be responsible to do it.

Having given these replies to him, one may still have an
awareness that Mr. Ramsey is right in at least one very important respect. Most of the argumentation about the morality
of nuclear warfare has not been, as it ought to be, addressed
to the question he insists upon: what should we regard, on our
own principles, as justifiable force?

8. A HAPPY DAY IN THE COUNTRY

January 9, 1961

On a beautiful Sunday in sunny California we piled the kids into the station wagon and tootled along on that big highway 101, with all these other station wagons, beside the blue Pacific. We went past Gaviota Beach and El Capitan Beach, filled with happy splashing crowds. Pretty soon we turned up through the hills, and drove past signs saying, first, "Watch Out For Deer," and then "52nd Missile Squadron — Peace Is Our Business" (California has everything: the ocean and the mountain, deer and missile squadrons). We came eventually out into this big flat parklike place, where the jet runways made ideal parking lots for the thousands of cars that were gathering. We joined these thousands of happy American families, with sport shirts, blankets, and cameras, at the first "open house" at Vandenberg Air Force Base. We were all going to get a look at our nation's "missile muscle."

The children played on the grass. We listened to the band, bought ice cream bars and Pepsi-Cola from the local Boy Scouts, and poked around in displays of the Titan missile. We climbed up into a new jet bomber. We were pled with to stay out of the center bleachers where only the Commanding General's personally invited guests were allowed, please. Spreading our rug, we sat on the ground to watch the entertainment. Varieties of fighters and bombers droned by in front of us in interesting formations and we clapped vigorously. Then the announcer said, "It is the pleasure of the 51st Munitions Maintenance Squadron to present a show, or, you might say, a demonstration — an explosive sequence; we hope you enjoy this demonstration, ladies and gentlemen." We watched cheerfully while there were shot off for us several highboys ("Let's hope we don't hit no Russian subs out there — because those are going outside the three-mile limit," joked the master of ceremonies, a jovial fellow with an Arkansas accent). As frolicking folk will, we got in the way of the program ("We will not detonate until everyone is back fifty feet; there are people or somebody in the area"). Finally as the *pièce de résistance* we had a "simulated atomic explosion," mushroom-cloud and all ("We hope to give you a big fireball"). It was quite a day: sort of a Kansas State Fair with glimpses of Hell.

Concluding Remarks:
Politics and American Values

OUR AMERICAN outlook on politics is peculiarly prone to an excessive idealism, and then to a disgusted, cynical reaction against it. Sometimes these two exist simultaneously. The man who is cynical about political life because his ideal expectations about it are altogether too high — or rather too naïve or "pure" or uncritical or uninformed — is by no means an unfamiliar phenomenon.

The 1950's saw much of the lofty suprapolitical side of this combination, and perhaps a little of the cynical underside, too. It is important to resist the sour and negative side, as well as the utopian side, of this combination, and to resist it whether it appears in the emotional backwash of the moralizer on the road back from his crusade, or in the excessive sensitivity and lack of persistence in the too easily discouraged purist, or in the shock of the provincial man discovering in politics that people differ, or in the implications-by-neglect of some hard-headed operators and scientific students of society, or, of course, in the ruthlessness of the genuine 100 percent cynic out to get his own in the jungle of life.

The cynic and the "above politics" man share a negative judgment on politics — the one to exploit, the other to pretend to escape its supposedly evil nature. But politics is a serious, worthy, important activity — not to be covered over with

glamour or romance, of course, but not to be regarded as ne-
farious, either. It is in part the struggle for power among
contending interests, yes, but the struggle takes place within
a frame of larger agreements (in the United States, fortu-
nately, a solid frame), and the power is sought for some purpose (in part, the shared purpose of running a state). The
self-interests are not altogether divorced from some goods for
the larger whole.

And the struggle for power among interests itself is not
necessarily a reprehensible thing; that depends upon what the
interests are and how the struggle is carried out. Power —
the ability to secure compliance — is a constant fact of social
life, and is not by nature a black, evil, nasty thing. Lord
Acton's excessively famous remark has at best only part of the
truth; having great power sometimes does corrupt a man's
character, but sometimes, with other men and other circumstances, it brings out some unexpected virtue and ability; one
rises to the occasion, as is often said of our American presidents. Perhaps *seeking* power more consistently corrupts men,
but even there it depends upon the man and the purposes for
which power is sought. There is, indeed, a form of human
corruption that is the love of power for its own sake, the perverse satisfaction in bending others to one's will. This corruption does, of course, appear in politics — but not only
there (husbands, wives, fathers, children, businessmen and
others, also have it) and it is not the only corruption to which
human character is subject. To name one other set, there is
irresponsibility, apathy, retreat, escape, soft hedonism, lazi-
ness, timidity, selfish disengagement, the lofty pretense to be
"above the battle." Being *without* power has its corrupting
effects, sometimes, too: men feel no responsibility, no link, no
identification with their society and its purposes and institutions, but ignore them, except perhaps to snarl at them. Then

there are those who *might* have power but do not seek it, or who do have it, but do not exercise it or who exercise it, but do not admit to themselves that they do, or who exercise power, but without political wisdom: are any of these admirable? American popular culture is plentifully supplied with negative notions about power and politics, politicians and the state: see almost any newspaper or man in the street. The state is a threat, the best government governs least, politicians are power-mad and without principle, public officials, "bureaucrats," civil servants receive little respect. We do not have a comparable set of negative notions for the people who pursue only private interest, or who retreat to the suburbs from the taxes and responsibilities and politics of the city — a city that they nevertheless want to use. We also do not have negative symbols for those who engage in politics naïvely because they have been taught not to believe in it. We do not have positive ideas about statecraft as a high and important human art, or about the statesman-politician as a worthy man.

The sins of irresponsibility may be as destructive as the sins of power, and in our American situation the former are more dangerous because less noted. We have power; the issue is how we will understand it and use it.

The "interests" that contend in politics are not necessarily reprehensible, either. The moralistic negation of politics rests in part on a too sharp separation of selfishness and altruism, and on illusions about the amount of the latter possible in ordinary life. The self-interest question is not the only moral question, and in collective life, especially, it is misleading to make it so: the additional questions, about the ends or goods that are served — whether for the self or "others" — should not be obscured. Usually in social life the self is a participant in a shared good sought for the community.

Not all "self-interested" activity is undesirable, and not all politics reduces to self-interest. One set of interests-and-values contends with another set of interests-and-values. We should not insist upon "pure" values, or "pure" disinterested service to the common good — the search for these (for a "moral crusade") is a source of our faulty view — but we should not fall, on the other side, into the safe cynicism of the hardboiled newspaper reporter's iron law of self-interest. These two mistaken views, apparently at opposite poles, really are connected to each other; they share a disdain for real political life.

But overarching the conflict and the power-seeking and the interest-serving of that life is something good: the community's effort to organize, shape, maintain, and perhaps improve itself; the perennial quest for justice and the common good. The America of the fifties did not serve that quest as well as it might have because, among other things, it did not yet quite admit that politics is a necessary and an honorable part of that quest.